JAMES McNAIR

Cooks
Italian

PHOTOGRAPHY AND STYLING BY JAMES McNAIR

CHRONICLE BOOKS

SAN FRANCISCO

Printed in Hong Kong.

Library of Congress
Cataloging-in-Publication Data
McNair, James K.
James McNair cooks Italian /
photography and styling by James McNair
p. cm.
Includes index
ISBN 0-8118-0424-0 (PB)
ISBN 0-8118-0449-6 (HB)
1. Cookery, Italian. I. Title
TX723.M397 1994
641.5945—dc20   93-45330
                                   CIP

Distributed in Canada by
Raincoast Books
112 East Third Avenue
Vancouver, British Columbia V5T 1C8

10 9 8 7 6 5 4 3 2 1

Chronicle Books
275 Fifth Street
San Francisco, California 94103

DEDICATION

For Ryan Stanton Richardson, my nephew, whose arrival into the world was perfectly timed to coincide with the completion of this volume. No doubt his first solid food will be Italian.

And in memory of Gregg King, who grew up a few years behind me as a protégé and who was valued as a brother and close friend.

Editorial and Photographic Production by James McNair and Andrew Moore
Villa Sunshine Books, Napa Valley, California.

Book design and Typography by Rick Dinihanian and John Lyle
Green Lizard Design, St. Helena, California.

With a few minor exceptions, all dishes, glassware, flatware, linens, and accessories are from Fillamento, San Francisco.
Backgrounds on the cover and on pages 87, 135, and 148 were painted by Ami Magill.
The author as Bacchus on page 11 and the back cover was painted by Alan May.
The title page illustration and chapter introduction backgrounds were painted by Michael Duté.

CONTENTS

I frequently glance out the kitchen window of my hillside home to take in the vineyards below. Whether clothed in summer greens or autumn bronzes, or standing naked and gray during the frosty winter months, they never cease to thrill me. Looking past the vineyards, to the little town of St. Helena and its surrounding lush hills outlined against the blue sky, I have to remind myself that I am in the Napa Valley in California, not in Tuscany in Italy.

Likewise, at my lakeside retreat, my kitchen window affords a stunning view. But there it is of clear blue water surrounded by lofty, snow-capped mountain peaks. Only the rustic wooden architecture and dry conifer forests jar me into the realization that I'm at Lake Tahoe, and not at the equally stunning Lake Como.

Although I cook Italian food in California, far from its Old World birthplace, and I am not Italian by heritage, I feel a spiritual connection to that special land crowded with spectacular scenery, amazing architecture and art treasures, and a rich culinary heritage.

My first encounter with Italian food, or rather Americanized Italian fare, was back in the days of long-simmered tomato sauces, meatballs and spaghetti, and heavy lasagna. In that bygone time, even packaged grated "parmesan" cheese tasted wonderfully exotic to the unexposed palate of a Louisiana lad. Over the years my love of Italian cuisine flourished, as I feasted on more authentic fare in New York's Little Italy and San Francisco's North Beach, and on the real thing in the mother country.

Like most aficionados of Italian cooking, I was first lured by the dishes of Italy because of their marvelous ingredients and the straightforward manner in which they are prepared, a manner that emphasizes and never masks natural flavors and textures. How can one go wrong when using garden-ripe vegetables, peak-of-the-season fruits, fresh herbs, real butter, fruity olive oil, exquisitely fresh fish and shellfish, and high-quality poultry and meat? This emphasis on simple cooking with the finest ingredients is what attracted many to the Italian table and what has played an important role in the style that came to be known as both new American cooking and California cuisine.

A volume of this size certainly cannot pretend to be a definitive book on the vast subject of Italian cooking, nor is it intended to be a record of authentic recipes from the many regions of Italy. It is, rather, my own collection of favorite Italian and Italian-inspired dishes not previously published.

Those of you who are familiar with my single-subject series are aware that most of those volumes include numerous Italian recipes; if bound together in a collection they would fill a volume considerably larger than this one. For your convenience, an index to those recipes is included at the end of this book.

In preparation for this volume, I returned to Italy to see if the national fare had changed since my last visit. I found that there is less emphasis on regional cooking, especially in the major cities where restaurants often feature dishes from all over the country. But there are still many restaurant chefs and home cooks who stick with the centuries-old fare of their surroundings.

It also seems that Italian-style dining is no longer bound by hard-and-fast rules. Up until a few years ago, most Italians worked their way through an appetizer (*antipasto*); a first course (*primo piatto*) of soup, pasta, risotto, polenta, or dumplings; a second course (*secondo piatto*) of fish, poultry, or meat accompanied or followed by a side dish (*contorno*); a salad (*insalata*); a cheese (*formaggio*); and, finally, fruit (*frutta*) or a special-occasion dessert (*dolce*).

Modern Italians frequently compose a meal of fewer dishes. Like many of us, they may choose to have only several appetizers, or a large portion of a traditional first course such as pasta, perhaps accompanied, preceded, or followed by a salad. I have also observed Italians who begin their meal with a tossed green salad instead of using the crisp greens to cleanse their palate after the meat course. And although the majority of diners still prefer to end their meal with a bowl of fresh fruit, reserving their pastry or other sweet as an afternoon treat, many restaurant patrons now opt to finish off with a rich dessert. Ice cream (*gelato*) continues to be savored in the afternoon or during the evening after-dinner stroll.

Traditionally, Italians begin their day with bread and coffee and take their large meal at midday, followed by an early afternoon rest break when all the shops and businesses are closed. The evening meal is a simpler affair, perhaps just a bowl of soup or a pasta. With the changing work habits, especially in bustling cities, many Italians are eating lighter lunches and reserving the bigger meal for the evening's entertainment.

Join me now in a very personal culinary sampling of one of the world's greatest cuisines.

BEGINNINGS

BEVERAGES

(*Bibite*)

—

APPETIZERS

(*Antipasti*)

—

FIRST COURSES

(*Primi piatti*)

*C*hoosing the best beverage to precede or accompany an Italian meal adds to the overall dining experience. I've included three of my favorite *aperitivi* as preludes, followed by a brief discussion of Italian wines. In addition to wine, every well-set Italian table includes the ubiquitous bottle of well-chilled mineral water (*aqua minerale*), with or without the sparkles.

Although the majority of Italians drink wine with their meals, if you prefer another beverage, consider alternatives that are still Italian in spirit: fresh fruit juice (*succo di frutta*), lemonade (*limonata*), orange soda (*aranciata*), and soft drinks made from Italian syrups, available in a wide range of flavors, stirred into sparkling water.

When most Americans hear the word *antipasto*, it conjures up an image of the platter loaded with cold cuts and marinated vegetables offered by so many Italian restaurants here. Italian home cooks are far more likely to put out one delicacy to tease the appetite, while Italian chefs may offer a wide range of tantalizing morsels, each served separately, from which diners assemble their own selections.

Once the appetizers are finished, the traditional meal begins. According to the region and sometimes the season, the first course is either a soup or a starch dish: pasta, risotto, polenta, or *gnocchi*. Only a few pasta dishes appear here, since many of my best pasta recipes are already in either my *Pasta Cookbook* or one of my other volumes.

Most Italians do not drink hard liquor and there is no cocktail hour. Instead, Italian-made sweet vermouth such as Cinzano or Martini or other light alcoholic beverages may be drunk throughout the day. Since many Americans enjoy a drink in the early evening, here are three aperitivi in the Italian mode that I enjoy serving on those rare occasions when I desire something other than a glass of wine or sparkling mineral water. ❧

CAMPARI SODA

Bitter Campari is an acquired taste. A little of the *aperitivo* with sparkling water always takes me back to a grapevine-covered taverna in Rome where I sipped my first glass of this ruby-colored beverage.

Ice cubes
1 ounce Campari
Well-chilled carbonated water or mineral water
Lemon slice (optional)

To make a Campari Soda, add ice cubes to a tumbler or a tall glass. Add the Campari and fill the glass with sparkling water. Add the lemon slice (if used).

NEGRONI

Fellow Napa Valley Italian food enthusiast Antonia Allegra introduced me to the Negroni, a blend of Italian Campari, vermouth, and gin. It is probably of American origin, yet it sets the proper tone for Italian dining.

Ice cubes
1 ounce gin
1 ounce Campari
1 ounce Italian sweet vermouth
Splash of carbonated water (optional)
Lemon peel twist

To make a Negroni, add ice cubes to a glass used for old-fashioneds or to a tumbler. In a cocktail shaker, combine the gin, Campari, vermouth, and more ice cubes. Shake to blend, then strain into the glass. Add the carbonated water (if used) and the lemon twist.

BELLINI

The Bellini was invented in the 1930s at Harry's Bar in Venice and named in honor of the artist Giovanni Bellini. When white peaches are in season, peel and stone ripe fruits and put them through a food mill. If the peaches are not very sweet, add Simple Syrup (page 141) to taste. Cover tightly and chill or freeze for later use. The purée is combined with Prosecco, a dry sparkling wine; substitute fruitier Spumante or a dry domestic sparkling wine if you can't locate Prosecco.

Ice cubes
1 ounce well-chilled white peach purée
3 ounces well-chilled Prosecco

To make a Bellini, fill a tall highball glass or a Champagne flute with ice. Let stand until the glass is chilled, then discard the ice. In a cocktail shaker, combine the chilled peach purée and the sparkling wine and shake to blend. Pour into the cold glass and serve immediately.

Each recipe makes 1 serving.

VINI

FAVORITE ITALIAN WINES

MELLOW WHITES. Est! Est! Est!, Frascati, Gavi di Gavi, Moscato d'Asti, Pinot Grigio.

DRY, MEDIUM-BODIED WHITES. Orvieto Secco, Soave, Verdicchio, Vernaccia di San Gimignano.

FRUITY, LIGHT-BODIED REDS. Bardolino, Valpolicella.

DRY, MEDIUM-BODIED REDS. Barbaresco, Chianti, Grignolino, Merlot, Nebbiolo, Nobile di Montepulciano.

HEARTY REDS. Barbera, Barolo, Brunello di Montalcino, Cabernet Franc, Chianti Classico, Gattinara.

DESSERT WINES. Marsala, Moscato, Vin Santo.

SPARKLING WINES. Asti Spumante (fruity), Prosecco (semidry), Spumante Brut (dry).

Italy is the world's most prolific wine-producing nation, creating a profusion of names and labels that can be confusing. A good wine merchant is the best source of current advice, but here are a few guidelines to help you select which wine to buy.

Italian wines may be named for the geographical location (Barolo, Chianti, or Orvieto), the name of the grape (Pinot Grigio or Riesling), the name of the grape coupled with the locale (Barbera d'Alba or Prosecco di Conegliano), or a brand or generic name (Corvo or Venegazzu).

When the words *Denominazione di Origine Controllata* or the letters *DOC* appear on the label, you can rest assured that the wine is from the area named, the vintage year is accurate, and production and aging methods have been carried out under the guidance of Italy's official wine-controlling body. Wines labeled *DOS* (*Denominazione Semplice*) are generally not as outstanding as those marked *DOC*, while labels bearing *DOCG*, or *Denominazione di Origine Controllata e Garantita*, indicate that the quality of the wine is guaranteed by the strictest governmental wine legislation in the world.

The word *Classico* can only appear on a label if the wine comes from the best or central part of the general area of production. Although this often indicates a very good wine, such is not always the case.

The words *Riserva, Riserva Speciale*, and *Riserva Superiore* indicate that the wines have been aged longer than the time that is considered normal and should be of higher quality than the same wines without these designations.

A small label affixed to the wine bottle may name the *consorzio*, or association of wine producers, responsible for producing the wine. Such a label does not guarantee quality, but may help you discover that you have a preference for wines produced by one *consorzio* over those of another.

One thing to keep in mind is that many Italian wines are made from grapes rarely grown elsewhere in the world, thus they are difficult to compare with wines from other countries. Finding the Italian wines that go best with Italian dishes is simply a matter of taste, so please enjoy the discovery.

ASSORTED APPETIZERS

On those occasions when you wish to serve a variety of appetizers followed by a simple meal, consider a presentation of assorted delicacies, both homemade and prepared. Arrange selected appetizers on a large platter or distribute among individual plates.

SUGGESTED ASSORTMENT
Sicilian Eggplant Relish (page 18)
Marinated Roasted Sweet Peppers (page 152)
Tuscan White Beans, Tomato Variation (page 101)
Sliced ripe tomatoes, topped with Basil Sauce, Genoa Style (page 154)
Grilled eggplant slices, brushed with extra-virgin olive oil
Seafood salads (use a favorite recipe or see index, page 164, for recipes in my other books)
Poached Veal in Tuna Sauce (see my book *Cold Cuisine*)
Hollowed-out cherry tomatoes stuffed with drained canned tuna or a favorite rice salad
Imported olives
Pickled vegetables
Breadsticks or other favorite Italian breads
Fried risotto balls made from leftover risotto (page 56)

ANTIPASTI ASSORTITI
ASSORTED APPETIZERS

*I*talian home cooks and professional chefs regularly buy good-quality commercially prepared products or delicatessen offerings for serving as appetizers. Canned tuna packed in olive oil is especially popular, as are anchovies, olives, and pickled vegetables.

One of my favorite parties expands the assorted platter to an antipasto table, a spread that is reminiscent of the mouthwatering displays placed seductively just inside the door of many Italian restaurants. I put out large platters and bowls of appetizers for guests to help themselves. Country bread and a great Italian wine, or an assortment of wines for tasting, round out an easy-to-assemble and festive evening.

SALUMI

SLICED CURED MEATS

One of the most common antipasti on the Italian table is a simple plate of one or more thinly sliced cured meats. Not long ago each region generally carried only their own locally produced products, but today in restaurants and salumerie you are likely to encounter an array of cured meats from all over Italy. These delectable cold cuts are usually served alone or just with crusty bread and perhaps butter or a drizzle of olive oil. Rarely are they offered with other types of antipasti.

In the photograph, I've combined slices of ham from Parma (*prosciutto*), Italian air-cured bacon (*pancetta*), two types of salami, and the dried beef counterpart to prosciutto called *bresaola*. Unfortunately, *bresaola* from Italy cannot presently be imported into the United States, but there are some fairly good domestic versions as well as Swiss products now available.

8 ounces thinly sliced cured meats, one type or a combination

Arrange the meat slices on individual dishes. Serve plain or with variations below.

Makes 4 servings.

VARIATIONS

To dress up the dish, shavings of Parmigiano-Reggiano or the leaves of greens such as arugula or basil may be scattered over the cold cuts. You might also set out lemon wedges and pass a pepper mill for topping off the meats to each diner's taste. Although the combination is more common in America than in Italy, cold cuts may be coupled with fresh fruits such as figs or sliced melon, papaya, or pears.

SLICED RAW BEEF

1 pound top-quality beef tenderloin, trimmed of all fat and connective tissue
About 3 ounces parmesan cheese, preferably Parmigiano-Reggiano
  cheese, in one piece
About 3 cups rinsed, dried, and chilled arugula or basil leaves
Extra-virgin olive oil
Red wine vinegar or lemon wedges

Quickly rinse the beef under running cold water and pat dry with paper toweling. Wrap in freezer wrap or plastic wrap and place in the freezer until the meat is very cold but not frozen hard, about 2 hours.

Shortly before serving, using an electric slicer or a very sharp knife, slice the beef across the grain as thinly as possible. Place a slice of beef between 2 sheets of waxed paper or plastic wrap and pound with a mallet or other flat, heavy instrument until the beef is as thin as possible; be careful that it does not tear. Remove the top sheet of paper or wrap, lift the bottom sheet, and place beef side down on an individual serving plate; peel off the remaining sheet of paper or wrap. Continue in the same manner, covering each plate with a single layer of beef slices.

Using a vegetable peeler, shave the cheese over the beef. Using a sharp knife, cut the arugula or basil into *chiffonade* strips or coarsely chop them. Strew the greens over the beef and cheese and serve immediately. Offer olive oil and vinegar or lemon wedges at the table.

Makes 6 servings.

CARPACCIO
SLICED RAW BEEF

*E*ven though I confess to being a bit wary about eating raw meat these days, I still occasionally indulge in this delicacy, which originated in Harry's Bar, a Venetian institution that has been frequented by celebrities and people watchers since it was popularized by Ernest Hemingway.

Be sure to buy the tenderest possible beef from a very reliable source. ❦

CAPONATA

SICILIAN EGGPLANT RELISH

This sweet-and-sour concoction may be made in quantity when the garden is at its peak and then preserved in jars for year-round enjoyment (see Note). When offering as an appetizer, serve alone, arrange on greens, spread atop crostini *(page 27) or* bruschetta *(page 31), or add to a mixed* antipasti *platter (page 13). It is also a tasty accompaniment to grilled fish, poultry, or meats, and makes an unusual sauce for hot or cold pasta.* ❧

SICILIAN EGGPLANT RELISH

6 tablespoons olive oil, preferably extra-virgin
2 pounds small or medium eggplants, peeled, if desired,
  and cut into 1-inch cubes
2 cups chopped yellow onion
1 cup chopped fennel or celery
1 cup chopped red sweet pepper
1 teaspoon minced or pressed garlic
2½ cups peeled, seeded, drained, and chopped ripe or canned tomato
¼ cup red wine vinegar
About 2 tablespoons sugar
About ½ teaspoon salt
About ¼ teaspoon freshly ground black pepper
¼ cup well-drained capers
6 Sicilian-style green olives, pitted and cut into quarters
¼ cup pine nuts
½ cup chopped fresh basil

In a sauté pan or skillet, heat 4 tablespoons of the olive oil over medium-high heat. Add the eggplant and sauté until soft and browned, about 10 minutes. Remove to a bowl and set aside.

Add the remaining 2 tablespoons olive oil to the same pan and place over medium-high heat. Add the onion, fennel or celery, and sweet pepper and sauté until soft, about 5 minutes. Stir in the garlic and cook for about 1 minute longer. Add the tomato, vinegar, browned eggplant, and sugar, salt, and pepper to taste. Bring the mixture to a boil, then reduce the heat to low and simmer uncovered, stirring frequently, for about 10 minutes.

Stir in the capers and olives and continue to simmer until the eggplant is tender, about 15 minutes longer. Taste and add more vinegar and/or sugar, salt, and pepper. Stir in the nuts and basil and simmer until heated through, about 5 minutes longer. Remove from the heat and let cool to room temperature before serving, or cool, cover, and refrigerate for as long as 2 weeks.

Makes 6 servings.

NOTE: To preserve the relish, ladle the hot mixture into sterilized jars. Seal and process in a boiling-water bath for 25 minutes, following canning-jar manufacturer's directions. Check the jars and store those with good seals in a cool, dark place for up to a year. Any jar that does not have a proper seal should be placed in the refrigerator and eaten within 2 weeks.

FRIED ARTICHOKES, JEWISH STYLE

Juice of 1 lemon
6 medium-sized young artichokes
Canola oil or other high-quality vegetable oil for deep-frying
Salt
Freshly ground black pepper

In a large bowl, pour in enough cold water to cover all of the artichokes once they are added. Squeeze in the lemon juice and set aside.

Cut off and discard the stems from the artichokes. Snap off the tough lower leaves. Then, using scissors, cut off the outer part of the remaining leaves, leaving only the pale greenish edible portion near the base of each leaf. As you work toward the choke, the edible portion becomes longer. When you reach the core of leaves in the center, using a knife, slice off the green tips. Then, using a spoon, scoop out and discard the fuzzy interior choke. Using a sharp knife or vegetable peeler, pare the lower part of the outside leaves near the base to expose the light green portion. As soon as each artichoke is trimmed, drop it into the lemon water to prevent darkening.

Pour the oil into a deep-fat fryer or deep pan to a depth of about 2 inches. Heat the electric fryer or place the pan over medium heat until the temperature reaches 300°F or until a small piece of bread dropped into the hot oil turns golden within about 30 seconds.

Meanwhile, remove the artichokes from the lemon water and pat dry with paper toweling. Gently spread the leaves out as much as possible without breaking them, then lay each artichoke, stem end up, on a work surface and flatten gently with your hand. Sprinkle inside and out with salt and pepper.

Working in batches if necessary to avoid overcrowding the pan, carefully drop the artichokes into the hot oil and cook, turning several times and pressing the artichokes against the bottom of the pan with a long-handled utensil to open up the leaves, until the bottoms pierce easily with a fork or wooden skewer, 8 to 10 minutes. Using a slotted utensil, transfer, stem end up, to paper toweling to drain well and press to flatten further and spread the leaves.

Increase the heat to 375°F or until a small piece of bread dropped into the hot oil turns brown within a few seconds. Return the artichokes to the oil and cook, turning almost constantly, until golden and crisp, about 3 minutes. For extra crispiness, sprinkle cold water into the hot oil during the last minute or so of cooking. Using a slotted utensil, transfer, stem end up, to paper toweling to drain briefly. Invert and serve piping hot or at room temperature.

Makes 6 servings.

CARCIOFI ALLA GIUDIA
FRIED ARTICHOKES, JEWISH STYLE

Although most commonly served as an antipasto, these golden beauties, which originated in Rome's Jewish ghetto, make a great accompaniment to a second course as well. They're also great with burgers! 🍒

BAGNA CAUDA
WARM ANCHOVY DIP

Bagna cauda *translates to "hot bath," an apt description of this warm anchovy-laced dip from Piedmont that is delicious served with garden-fresh produce. While holding a piece of bread in one hand, use the other hand to dunk vegetables into the "bath," then use the bread to catch drips enroute to your mouth. Of course, no one can resist dunking the bread into the aromatic dip from time to time.* ❧

22

Vegetables for dipping can be washed, dried, wrapped, and refrigerated for several hours before serving. Some cooks prefer to serve vegetables that have been steamed until crisp-tender, then quickly chilled in iced water to preserve their color; be sure they are well drained before serving. Whenever possible leave vegetables whole; cut larger vegetables into bite-sized pieces. Choose whatever vegetables are in season and at their peak of flavor. Among my favorites for dipping are asparagus tips, broccoli and cauliflower florets, carrots, edible-pod peas, radishes, and red or gold sweet peppers. To make this dish authentically Italian, include slices of fennel and small, sweet cardoons or just the hearts from larger, tougher ones.

About 6 cups raw or steamed vegetables (see recipe introduction)
¼ cup olive oil, preferably extra-virgin
¾ cup (1½ sticks) unsalted butter
2 teaspoons minced or pressed garlic
1 can (2 ounces) anchovy fillets, drained and minced
Salt
Crusty country bread, sliced

Prepare the vegetables as described in the recipe introduction. Set aside.

In a small saucepan, heat the oil and butter over medium heat until the butter begins to foam. Add the garlic and sauté for about 1 minute; do not allow it to color. Add the anchovies, reduce the heat to low, and simmer, stirring constantly, until the anchovies fall apart, about 5 minutes. Add salt to taste.

At the table, pour the sauce into a container placed over a candle or other warming device. Alternatively, pour the hot dip into a heatproof serving container. Arrange the vegetables and bread slices alongside the dip.

Makes 8 servings.

ITALIAN OMELET

FRITTATA
ITALIAN OMELET

*W*hen I make frittata *for a large*

group, I triple this recipe, pour it into

a 9- by 13-inch ovenproof dish, and

bake it in a 350°F oven until set, then

cut it into bite-sized pieces and

arrange them on a serving tray. ❦

6 eggs, lightly beaten
2 tablespoons light cream or half-and-half
¼ cup freshly grated parmesan cheese (about 1 ounce), preferably
   Parmigiano-Reggiano
About 1 teaspoon salt
About ½ teaspoon freshly ground black pepper
1 tablespoon olive oil, preferably extra-virgin
1 tablespoon unsalted butter
½ cup minced yellow or red onion
1 teaspoon minced or pressed garlic (optional)
1½ cups sliced, shredded, or chopped summer squash, steamed or
   sautéed in olive oil until tender
About ¾ cup chopped summer squash blossoms (optional)
Minced mixed fresh herbs such as chervil, chives, basil or tarragon, and
   parsley, preferably flat-leaf type
Summer squash blossoms for garnish (optional)

In a bowl, combine the eggs, cream, cheese, and salt and pepper to taste. Beat until well blended. Set aside.

In a heavy-bottomed 10-inch skillet, preferably nonstick, heat the olive oil and butter over medium heat. When the butter stops foaming, add the onion and sauté until soft but not browned, about 5 minutes. Add the garlic (if used) and sauté for 1 minute longer.

Distribute the squash and the chopped squash blossoms (if used) evenly in the pan, then pour the egg mixture over the squash. Reduce the heat to low and cook undisturbed until the eggs are set around the edges. Using a spatula, gently lift the edges of the *frittata* and tilt the pan to let any uncooked egg run down under the bottom. Continue cooking until the eggs have almost set on top.

Invert a plate over the top of the pan and then invert the pan and plate together, so the *frittata* is on the plate. Slide the *frittata* back into the pan with the cooked side up. Cook until the bottom is set, 1 to 2 minutes. Alternatively, do not turn the *frittata*. Instead, place it under a preheated broiler until the top is set and tinged with brown, about 30 seconds; be sure that you are using a flameproof pan and be careful not to burn or overcook the *frittata*.

Again, invert a flat serving plate over the pan, invert them together, and turn the *frittata* out onto the serving plate. Or, if you have finished the frittata in a broiler, loosen the edges with a spatula and slide the *frittata* onto the plate. Sprinkle with the herb mixture, garnish with the squash blossoms (if used), and serve immediately, or cool to room temperature before serving. To serve, cut into wedges.

Makes 4 servings.

Variations on page 26.

ITALIAN OMELET VARIATIONS

Substitute any favorite vegetable or combination of vegetables for the squash.

Before adding the olive oil and butter to the pan, cook about 6 ounces American-style smoked bacon or Italian bacon (*pancetta*) until crisp. Transfer to paper toweling to drain; discard the bacon drippings. Crumble the bacon and sprinkle it over the cooked vegetables before pouring on the egg mixture.

Add 6 canned anchovy fillets, minced, or to taste, to the egg mixture.

Omit the vegetables. Distribute a layer of leftover cooked spaghetti or other pasta over the onion and garlic.

Omit the vegetables. Add 4 more eggs and ¼ cup minced fresh herb(s) of choice to the egg mixture.

For a lower-cholesterol *frittata*, use only the whites from 9 eggs instead of the 6 whole eggs.

CROUTON SANDWICHES

CHICKEN LIVER SPREAD
2 tablespoons olive oil or unsalted butter
1 cup chopped yellow onion
1 pound chicken livers, trimmed
¾ cup hearty red wine such as Barbera or Barolo
¼ cup homemade chicken broth or canned reduced-sodium chicken broth
1 canned anchovy fillet, drained and minced
1 tablespoon well-drained capers
1 tablespoon minced fresh sage, or 1 teaspoon crumbled dried sage
2 tablespoons tomato paste
Salt
Freshly ground black pepper

8 slices coarse, country-style white bread
Olive oil, preferably extra-virgin, for brushing on bread
Freshly grated parmesan cheese, preferably Parmigiano-Reggiano,
   for sprinkling
Tiny fresh sage leaves or flat-leaf parsley sprigs for garnish

To make the Chicken Liver Spread, in a sauté pan or skillet, heat the olive oil or butter over medium heat. Add the onion and sauté until soft but not browned, about 5 minutes. Add the chicken livers and sauté, breaking them up with a wooden spoon or cooking fork as they cook, until lightly colored, about 3 minutes. Stir in the wine, stock or broth, anchovy, capers, and minced or dried sage. Cook, stirring frequently, until the liquid evaporates, about 5 minutes.

Preheat an oven to 350°F.

Stir the tomato paste into the liver mixture and season with salt and pepper to taste. Cook, stirring frequently, until the livers are very soft, about 15 minutes. Transfer to a food processor fitted with a metal blade and blend until fairly smooth; alternatively, transfer to a bowl and whisk until blended. Cover and keep warm.

While the livers are cooking, begin the *crostini*. Cut the crusts from the bread slices and trim each slice into geometric shapes, creating 2 to 4 pieces from each slice. Brush lightly with olive oil on each side and place on a pizza screen or baking sheet. Bake, turning once, until crisp and golden brown on both sides, about 10 minutes on each side.

Spread the warm toasts with the warm liver mixture, sprinkle with a little cheese, and garnish with the sage. Serve warm.

Makes 8 servings.

Variations on page 28.

CROSTINI ASSORTITI
CROUTON SANDWICHES

*M*y recipe for chicken liver spread, shown on the square toast, is adapted from an Italian classic. Other topping choices include a blend of white beans and tuna, shown on the triangular bread, and puréed artichoke, parmesan cheese, and anchovy. Recipes for these and other variations follow. ❧

Artichoke Topping (*Crostini al carciofo*). In a food processor fitted with a metal blade, combine about 1½ cups cooked fresh artichoke hearts (or one 13-ounce can artichoke hearts, drained); ¾ cup freshly grated parmesan cheese (about 3 ounces), preferably Parmigiano-Reggiano; and 1 canned anchovy fillet. Blend well. Add about 2 tablespoons homemade mayonnaise (page 155) or good commercial mayonnaise, or enough to moisten the mixture to taste. Blend well. Season to taste with salt. Spread on warm toasts and garnish with anchovy fillets rolled around capers.

White Beans and Tuna Topping (*Crostini al fagioli e tonno*). In a small skillet, heat 1 tablespoon olive oil over medium heat. Add 1 cup chopped yellow onion and sauté, stirring frequently, until soft but not browned, about 5 minutes. Stir in 2 teaspoons minced or pressed garlic and sauté for about 1 minute longer. Transfer to a food processor fitted with a metal blade. Add 1 cup drained Tuscan White Beans (page 100) and 1 can (6 ounces) tuna (preferably packed in olive oil), drained, and process until fairly smooth. Stir in about 2 tablespoons freshly squeezed lemon juice, or to taste, and season with salt and freshly ground black pepper to taste. Spread on warm toasts and garnish with small arugula or basil leaves and strips of roasted sweet red pepper (page 152).

Cheese and Tomato Topping (*Crostini al formaggio e pomodoro*). Top warm toasts with slices of fresh mozzarella. Sprinkle with chopped fresh tomato or drained, oil-packed, sun-dried tomato, and salt to taste. Arrange on a baking sheet and place in a preheated 350°F oven until the cheese just begins to melt. Serve warm.

28

GARLIC TOAST WITH TOMATO AND BASIL

1 cup peeled, seeded, chopped, and drained ripe tomato
¼ cup chopped fresh basil
Salt
Olive oil, preferably extra-virgin
Vegetable oil for brushing on grill rack
6 slices coarse-textured Italian or French bread, about ½ inch thick
4 garlic cloves, lightly smashed
Freshly ground black pepper

Prepare an open grill for moderate direct-heat cooking or preheat a broiler.

To prepare the topping, in a bowl, combine the tomato, basil, and salt to taste. Drizzle with just enough olive oil to moisten. Toss to blend well. Set aside, do not refrigerate.

When the fire or broiler is ready, lightly brush the grill rack with vegetable oil. Add the bread slices and cook, turning once, until toasted to your preference. Rub the warm bread with the garlic, then brush or drizzle generously with olive oil and sprinkle with salt and pepper to taste. Spoon the tomato mixture over the toast and serve at once.

Makes 6 servings.

VARIATIONS

After turning the bread the first time, drizzle the slices with olive oil and move the bread to a cooler part of the grill to keep the bottom from burning. Top each bread slice with a thick slice of Fontina or other good-melting cheese at room temperature. Grill until the cheese melts. Remove from the grill and spoon on the tomato mixture or dollops of caramelized onion (page 39).

Omit the tomato mixture. Top the grilled bread with Sicilian Eggplant Relish (page 18) or a mixture of chopped Italian-style olives, capers, minced fresh basil, and olive oil. Sprinkle the latter topping with freshly grated parmesan cheese, preferably Parmigiano-Reggiano.

Top one half of each slice with drained Tuscan White Beans (page 101) and the other half with sautéed spinach.

BRUSCHETTA O FETT'UNTA CON POMODORO E BASILICO

GARLIC TOAST WITH TOMATO AND BASIL

This toast, a more rustic version of crostini, is also quite delicious without the tomato-basil topping. Or top the hot bread with any of the variations for crostini (page 28). ❧

*PANINI CON PANCETTA,
RUCOLA, E POMODORO*

PANCETTA, ARUGULA, AND TCMATO
SANDWICHES

*My Italian variation on the BLT
could well be dubbed a PAT.
Garden-ripe summer tomatoes are
essential for the success of this
sandwich. Pungent arugula and
peppery pancetta team with chewy
focaccia for a sensational
combination, all bound together by
garlicky mayonnaise. Basil leaves
offer a delicious alternative for those
who are sensitive to arugula, or
cannot locate or grow it.*

*Prepare small sandwiches or make
larger ones and cut them into sections
for serving as an antipasto or offer
them whole as a light meal.* ❦

PANCETTA, ARUGULA, AND TOMATO SANDWICHES

**Flatbread (page 160) or a 9-by-13-inch sheet high-quality commercial
flatbread (*focaccia*)**
Mayonnaise, Garlic Variation (page 155)
**1 pound Italian bacon (*pancetta*), sliced about the same thickness as you
prefer American bacon**
About 12 ripe tomato slices
2 to 3 cups arugula leaves

If you are making the bread, prepare it several hours in advance. If you are
purchasing it, set aside.

Prepare the Garlic Mayonnaise, cover, and refrigerate until needed.

In a skillet, fry the *pancetta* over medium heat until crisp. Using a slotted utensil,
transfer the *pancetta* to paper toweling to drain.

Cut the bread into 6 equal portions, then slice each piece in half horizontally.
Spread the cut sides of the bread with the mayonnaise. Arrange the tomato slices
on the bottom half of each section of bread and then layer with the *pancetta* and
then the arugula. Top with the other half of the bread sections, cut side down. Serve
immediately.

Makes 6 servings.

BREAD AND TOMATO SALAD

10 ounces stale Italian bread, sliced about ¾ inch thick
3 to 4 cups chopped ripe tomato, peeled and seeded if desired
1 cup minced red onion
1 teaspoon minced garlic
1 cup packed fresh basil leaves, torn if large
½ cup extra-virgin olive oil
About 3 tablespoons red wine vinegar
Salt
Freshly ground black pepper
Fresh basil sprigs for garnish

In a large bowl, place the bread and add cold water to cover. Set aside for about 20 minutes.

Drain off the water from the bread. Using your hands, squeeze out as much water as possible from the soaked bread and crumble it into a bowl. Add the tomato, onion, garlic, and basil leaves and toss to mix well. Pour the olive oil over the salad and add vinegar, salt, and pepper to taste. Toss thoroughly. Garnish with basil sprigs and serve immediately. Or omit the chopped basil and the garnish, cover, and chill for up to 2 hours; return to room temperature, then toss with the chopped basil and garnish just before serving.

Makes 8 servings.

PANZANELLA
BREAD AND TOMATO SALAD

Almost nothing is wasted in the Italian kitchen, and here is a wonderful use of stale bread, usually eaten as an antipasto or as a first course. The addition of cooked beans, fish, poultry, or meats, or drained canned tuna turns the simple salad into a complete meal. Some Italian cooks toss in chopped cucumber, sweet peppers, celery, anchovy fillets, hard-cooked eggs, grated parmesan, or other favorite salad additions. No matter what else you choose to add, flavorful vine-ripened tomatoes are absolutely essential.

Seeded or herbed Italian bread adds a nice touch to the salad. ❦

PANZAROTTI
DEEP-FRIED PIZZA POCKETS

One evening on our way to dinner at a fancy Milan restaurant, Andrew and I stumbled upon a hole-in-the-wall shop featuring these mouth-watering pies. Lines of people waited for the pies to come out of the hot oil. As each one was ready, the southern-Italian proprietor wrapped it in a section of waxed paper for eating out of hand. We decided to share one as an antipasto *before continuing on to the restaurant. But we ended up returning to the little shop and dining on several of these scrumptious* panzarotti *while window shopping on nearby via Montenapolecni. It turned into one of our most memorable meals in all of Italy.* ❧

Flatbread dough (page 160), or use a favorite recipe for pizza dough or purchase about 2 pounds fresh dough from a pizzeria
2 cups freshly shredded mozzarella cheese (about 8 ounces), preferably freshly made at a nearby source or imported from Italy
½ cup freshly grated parmesan cheese (about 2 ounces), preferably Parmigiano-Reggiano
¾ cup peeled, seeded, drained, and coarsely chopped ripe or canned tomato
¼ cup chopped fresh basil, 2 tablespoons chopped fresh oregano, or 1 tablespoon crumbled dried oregano
Salt
Olive oil for deep-frying

If you are making the dough, prepare it as directed and set aside to rise for about 1 hour. If using purchased dough that has already risen, cover and set aside while you prepare the filling.

In a bowl, combine the cheeses; set aside.

Divide the risen dough into 8 equal portions. Roll out each portion to form a round about 5 inches in diameter. Brush the rounds all over with olive oil. Using half of the cheese mixture, divide it equally among the rounds, covering half of each dough round with the mixture and leaving a ½-inch border around the edges. Sprinkle the tomato, basil or oregano, and salt to taste evenly over the cheese. Top the tomato with the remaining cheese mixture, again dividing it equally. Moisten the exposed edges of the dough with water, fold the uncovered side over the filling, and press the edges of the dough together to seal well. Using a wooden skewer or fork, punch several holes along the side opposite the sealed side to allow steam to escape during cooking.

Meanwhile, in a deep-fat fryer or deep pot such as a dutch oven, pour in olive oil to a depth of 2 inches and heat to 360°F, or until a small piece of dough or bread dropped into the hot oil turns golden within a few seconds. Carefully slip the *panzarotti*, a few at a time to avoid overcrowding, into the hot oil and cook, turning frequently, until golden, about 5 minutes. Using a slotted utensil, transfer to paper toweling to drain well. Serve piping hot.

Makes 8 servings.

VARIATIONS

Add other ingredients such as chopped prosciutto, olives, or sun-dried tomatoes to the filling. Or use any good-melting cheese in place of the mozzarella.

ONION SOUP, FLORENTINE STYLE

¼ cup olive oil, preferably extra-virgin
4 pounds yellow onions, cut in half lengthwise, then thinly sliced
2 teaspoons sugar
Salt
1 bottle (750 ml) dry white wine
4 cups Italian-Style Broth (page 157), made from chicken or meat, or 3 cups
    canned chicken or vegetable broth, preferably reduced-sodium type, diluted
    with 1 cup water
1 piece cinnamon stick, about 1½ inches long
4 cups torn or cut very stale Italian or French bread (about 5 ounces)
Whole fresh chives for garnish (optional)
Freshly grated parmesan cheese, preferably Parmigiano-Reggiano, for serving

In a heavy soup pot or dutch oven, heat the oil over medium heat. Add the onions
and toss to coat with the oil. Cover tightly, reduce the heat to medium-low, and
cook, stirring occasionally, until the onions are soft and just beginning to color,
about 30 minutes.

Remove the cover, increase the heat to medium, and cook, stirring occasionally,
until the onions are amber, about 45 minutes. Sprinkle with the sugar and a little
salt. Cook, stirring frequently, until the sugar melts and the onions are caramelized,
about 5 minutes longer. Add the wine, broth, and cinnamon stick. Stir well and
bring to a boil. Cover tightly, reduce the heat to low, and simmer gently, stirring
occasionally, for 1 hour.

Add the bread to the simmering soup and continue cooking, uncovered, until the
bread disintegrates, 30 to 45 minutes longer. Stir occasionally to prevent the soup
from sticking to the bottom of the pot.

Discard the cinnamon stick. Using a wire whisk, whip the soup until the bread is
well incorporated. Taste and add more salt if needed. Garnish with chives (if used)
and serve immediately or, preferably, let cool to room temperature, then cover and
refrigerate overnight. Slowly reheat before serving, or return to room temperature
for serving on a hot day. Pass the cheese at the table.

Makes 4 to 6 servings.

CARABACCIA
ONION SOUP, FLORENTINE STYLE

Carabaccia, *sometimes spelled
carabazada, has been served in
Florence since the Middle Ages. The
name translates to "a combination of
simple things," which is exactly what
goes into this thick soup. Like many
soups, this one tastes better when
made a day ahead and reheated.
Although usually eaten hot, this
hearty soup is often presented at
room temperature on warm summer
days.*

*For good caramelization, choose
onions that are somewhat dry.
Freshly picked onions contain so
much water that they fall apart by
the time they achieve good color.*

39

ZUPPA CREMA DI PEPERONI

CREAMY SWEET PEPPER SOUP

*F*or an attractive presentation,
make two batches of this creamy—
yet creamless—soup, one with red
peppers and the other with yellow
peppers. Ladle one color soup into
warmed soup bowls to fill halfway,
then ladle the second soup into the
center of the first soup. Draw a
wooden skewer through the top of the
soup to achieve an interesting
pattern.

CREAMY SWEET PEPPER SOUP

4 large red or yellow sweet peppers
2 tablespoons unsalted butter
1 cup chopped yellow onion
1 large baking potato (about 8 ounces), peeled and chopped
6 cups Italian-Style Broth (page 157), made from chicken or meat, or
    4 cups canned chicken or vegetable broth, preferably reduced-sodium type,
    diluted with 2 cups water
2 fresh thyme sprigs
2 bay leaves
Salt
Freshly ground white pepper
Extra-virgin olive oil for serving (optional)
Freshly grated parmesan cheese, preferably Parmigiano-Reggiano, for serving

Roast, peel, and seed the peppers as directed on page 152; do not add marinade ingredients. Coarsely chop and set aside.

In a heavy-bottomed saucepan, melt the butter over medium heat. Add the onion and cook, stirring frequently, until soft but not browned, about 5 minutes. Add the potato and broth, increase the heat to high, bring to a boil, and cook for 15 minutes. Reduce the heat to low. Tie the thyme and bay leaves in a cheesecloth bag and add to the simmering soup. Add the roasted peppers and cook until the potatoes are falling apart and creamy, about 45 minutes longer; add more broth or water if the soup becomes too thick.

Discard the bag of herbs. Working in batches if necessary, transfer the soup to a food processor fitted with a metal blade or to a blender and purée until smooth. Transfer the soup to a bowl and season with salt and pepper to taste. Serve hot, or cool slightly, then cover and refrigerate for as long as 2 days; slowly reheat before serving.

To serve, ladle the soup into warmed individual bowls, drizzle with olive oil (if used), and sprinkle with the cheese.

Makes 4 servings.

ZUPPA DI PESCE

FISH SOUP

*C*ountless versions of fish soup can be found all over Italy. Shrimp, scallops, or other shellfish may be combined with the fish pieces in this simple yet satisfying version. ❦

42

2 pounds trimmings, including skin and bones, from white-fleshed fish such as cod, red snapper, or sole
2 ripe or canned tomatoes, quartered
2 lemons, quartered
4 cups water
6 slices Italian bread, about ½ inch thick
Extra-virgin olive oil for brushing on bread
2 tablespoons olive oil
2 tablespoons unsalted butter
1 cup minced shallot or red onion
½ cup chopped celery or fennel
1 teaspoon minced or pressed garlic
2 pounds firm-fleshed fish fillet such as halibut, sea bass, tuna, or sturgeon, cut into large bite-sized pieces
1 cup peeled, seeded, drained, and chopped ripe or canned plum tomato
1 cup dry white wine
Salt
Freshly ground black pepper
Hot-pepper sauce such as Tabasco
About 2 tablespoons freshly squeezed lemon juice
Minced fresh parsley, preferably flat-leaf type, or basil for garnish
Lemon wedges for serving

Quickly rinse the white-fleshed fish under cold running water. Place in a stockpot or large saucepan. Add the quartered tomatoes and lemons and the water. Place over medium heat and bring to a simmer. Poach, uncovered, until the fish is very tender, about 30 minutes.

Remove from the heat. Strain the poaching liquid through a sieve lined with dampened cheesecloth into a bowl; reserve. Discard the fish, tomato, and lemons left in the sieve.

Preheat an oven to 350°F. Brush the bread slices on both sides with olive oil, place on a baking sheet, and toast in the oven until golden brown and crisp, about 25 minutes.

Meanwhile, in a clean stockpot or large saucepan, combine the oil and butter and place over medium heat. When the butter stops foaming, add the shallot or onion and celery or fennel and sauté until soft but not browned, about 5 minutes. Add the garlic and sauté for about 1 minute longer. Add the firm-fleshed fish pieces, chopped tomato, wine, reserved poaching liquid, and a little salt and pepper. Bring to a simmer over medium heat, then reduce the heat to low, cover, and continue to simmer until the fish pieces are tender but still hold their shape, about 10 minutes. Taste and add salt, pepper, pepper sauce, and lemon juice to taste.

To serve, place the toasted bread in warmed individual bowls and ladle the soup over the bread. Sprinkle with minced parsley or basil and serve immediately. Offer lemon wedges at the table.

Makes 6 servings.

CRESPELLE CON CIPOLLA E PATATA

ONION-AND-POTATO-FILLED PANCAKES

*F*or this dish, thin pancakes, called crespelle, *are filled and folded like* handkerchiefs, or fazzoletti, *which these folded pancakes are also sometimes called.* ❧

1 pound boiling (waxy) potatoes
6 tablespoons (¾ stick) unsalted butter
1 cup finely chopped yellow onion
1 teaspoon minced or pressed garlic
¼ cup light cream or half-and-half
Salt
Freshly ground black pepper
Additional light cream or half-and-half, heated, if needed

PANCAKES (*CRESPELLE*)
1¼ cups milk
1 cup all-purpose flour
Pinch of salt
3 eggs
Unsalted butter for cooking *crespelle*

Softened unsalted butter for greasing skillet and baking dish, plus
  2 tablespoons unsalted butter, melted
⅓ cup reduced Italian-Style Broth (page 157) or canned chicken or vegetable
  broth, preferably reduced-sodium type
Fresh parsley sprigs, preferably flat-leaf type, for garnish

Wash the potatoes under cold running water, scrubbing well to remove all traces of soil. Place them in a saucepan and add water to cover by about 4 inches, then remove the potatoes. Bring the water to a boil over medium-high heat, add the potatoes, and cook until just tender when pierced with a wooden skewer or small, sharp knife, 35 to 45 minutes.

Meanwhile, in a heavy-bottomed sauté pan or skillet, melt the butter over medium heat. Add the onion and cook, stirring frequently, until golden and very soft, about 8 minutes. Add the garlic and sauté for about 1 minute longer. Stir in the cream and heat through. Set aside.

Drain the potatoes, return them to the pan over medium heat, and shake the pan until any excess moisture evaporates and potatoes are dry to the touch. Remove from the heat and, as soon as the potatoes are cool enough to handle, peel and cut into chunks. Press the hot potatoes through a ricer into a large bowl. Stir in the reserved onion mixture and salt and pepper to taste; be generous with the pepper. Using a wooden spoon or wire whisk, whip the potatoes until light and fluffy, adding additional warm cream if required to form desired consistency; avoid making the potatoes too thin. Set aside.

Recipe continues on page 46.

44

a fine-mesh sieve or a *chinois* positioned over a clean saucepan and push the mixture through with a wooden spoon. Stir in the minced arugula and set aside. The sauce may be prepared up to 2 hours in advance, covered, refrigerated, and reheated.

Using a hand-cranked pasta machine, roll out the dough, gradually decreasing the settings to the second-thinnest position, or, using a rolling pin, roll out thinly. Using a knife or pastry wheel, cut the pasta into 3-inch squares. Place about 1 teaspoon of the filling in the center of each square. Brush the dough all around the filling with cold water. Fold the squares over to form triangles, and press down firmly around the mounds of filling to seal the pasta. If desired, trim the sealed edges with a fluted pastry wheel. Set aside on a clean cloth towel. (Reserve any leftover pasta dough for another purpose.)

In a large pot, bring the water to a rapid boil over high heat. While the water is coming to a boil, reheat the sauce over low heat. Stir the 1 tablespoon salt into the boiling water. Add the pasta and cook, stirring frequently, until tender, 1 to 2 minutes. Drain the pasta well and transfer to a warmed bowl. Spoon about half of the warmed sauce over the pasta and toss gently. Arrange the pasta on warmed individual plates, spoon the remaining sauce over the top, garnish with arugula leaves, and serve immediately.

Makes 6 to 8 servings.

SPAGHETTI WITH GARLIC AND OLIVE OIL

4 quarts water
½ cup extra-virgin olive oil
1 tablespoon minced garlic, or to taste
3 anchovy fillets, drained and minced (optional)
Salt
¾ pound imported Italian spaghetti
Freshly ground black pepper or crushed dried hot chile
2 tablespoons minced fresh parsley, preferably flat-leaf type
Freshly grated Parmigiano-Reggiano cheese for serving

In a large pot, bring the water to a rapid boil over high heat.

Meanwhile, in a heavy-bottomed sauté pan or skillet, combine the oil, garlic, and anchovies (if used) over low heat and cook until the garlic just begins to take on a hint of color; do not brown the garlic or it will turn bitter. Remove from the heat.

When the water boils, stir in 1 tablespoon salt. Drop the spaghetti into the boiling water and cook, stirring frequently, until tender but still firm to the bite. Timing will depend upon the brand; refer to the manufacturer's directions as a starting point, but begin to taste test the spaghetti before the time listed on the package. Drain well and transfer to the pan holding the garlicky olive oil. Toss well and season to taste with salt and black pepper or chile flakes.

Divide evenly among individual pasta dishes. Sprinkle each portion with parsley, crown lavishly with the cheese, and serve immediately.

Makes 4 servings.

SPAGHETTI AGLIO E OLIO
SPAGHETTI WITH GARLIC AND OLIVE OIL

My variation on this old Roman specialty has long been comfort food to me, so it had to have a place in my book of Italian favorites. It's quick, easy, and very satisfying, making it a great supper after working too long or when there's little time for cooking.

This is one dish in which I take on any number of Italian cooks and authors. Most brown the garlic in the oil, then discard it; I use a more gentle hand in cooking the garlic so that it never browns and adds bitterness and I leave it in the oil for added flavor. And for some unexplained reason that I fail to comprehend, the Italians serve this dish without any cheese. I much prefer my California version, which is showered with the world's finest cheese. ❦

CANNELLONI AL POLLO CON SALSA DI FUNGHI

CHICKEN-STUFFED PASTA ROLLS IN MUSHROOM SAUCE

Classic cannelloni require fresh pasta dough that is rolled very thinly, rather than the more easily made crêpes used by many American cooks. I've included a lighter sauce than the traditional one, which is laden with heavy cream and cheese. If you prefer to pursue the richer route, make the White Sauce with cream and add a cup or two of shredded Fontina. ❧

52

Fresh Pasta Dough (page 153)

CHICKEN STUFFING
2 tablespoons olive oil
1 cup finely chopped red onion
3 boned and skinned chicken breast halves (about 12 ounces total), coarsely chopped
4 ounces sliced prosciutto, chopped
2 tablespoons minced fresh parsley, preferably flat-leaf type
1 cup freshly shredded Italian Fontina cheese (about 5 ounces)
½ cup ricotta cheese (about 4 ounces)
Salt
Freshly ground black pepper

2 tablespoons unsalted butter
4 ounces fresh mushrooms, finely chopped
White Sauce (page 159)
½ cup freshly grated parmesan cheese (about 2 ounces), preferably Parmigiano-Reggiano
Finely chopped ripe tomato for garnish
Minced fresh parsley, preferably flat-leaf type, for garnish

Prepare the pasta dough as directed and set aside to rest for 2 hours.

Meanwhile, to make the stuffing, in a sauté pan or heavy skillet, heat the olive oil over medium-high heat. Add the onion and sauté until soft but not browned, about 5 minutes. Add the chicken and prosciutto and sauté until the chicken is done, about 5 minutes. Transfer the mixture to a food processor fitted with a metal blade and chop finely. Transfer to a bowl and stir in the parsley, Fontina and ricotta cheeses, and salt and pepper to taste. Cover and refrigerate until the pasta is ready for stuffing.

In a sauté pan or heavy skillet, melt the butter over medium-high heat. Add the mushrooms and sauté for about 2 minutes. Reduce the heat to medium-low and cook until tender, about 8 minutes longer.

Meanwhile, prepare the White Sauce as directed. Stir the mushrooms into the white sauce; set aside to cool slightly, then cover and refrigerate until needed.

Using a hand-cranked pasta machine, roll out the dough, gradually decreasing the settings to the second-thinnest position, or, using a rolling pin, roll out thinly. Cut out eight to ten 4-inch squares, dust lightly with flour, and set aside to dry for about 10 minutes. (Reserve any leftover pasta dough for another purpose.)

Recipe continues on page 54.

Fill a large pot three-fourths full of water and bring to a rapid boil over high heat. Drop the pasta squares, a few at a time, into the boiling water and cook for about 2 minutes. Using a wire utensil, transfer the pasta squares to a colander and rinse under cold running water. Place the pasta squares flat on a clean cloth towel to drain well. Parboil the remaining pasta in the same way.

Preheat an oven to 350°F.

Gently reheat the sauce over low heat. Spread half of the sauce in the bottom of a 9-by-13-inch baking dish. Spoon about 3 tablespoons of the stuffing mixture down the middle of each pasta square. Roll up each square into a cylinder and place, seam side down, in the baking dish, arranging the rolls in rows. Cover with the remaining sauce and sprinkle with the parmesan cheese. Bake uncovered until heated through and the sauce is bubbly, about 15 minutes.

Transfer the cannelloni to warmed individual plates. Garnish with tomato and parsley and serve immediately.

Makes 4 servings.

Basic Risotto with Parmesan Cheese

1½ cups short-grain Italian rice such as Arborio, Carnaroli, or Vialone Nano
About 5 cups Italian-Style Broth (page 157), made from chicken or veal, or
    5 cups canned chicken or vegetable broth, preferably reduced-sodium type
5 tablespoons unsalted butter
½ cup chopped yellow onion
1 teaspoon minced or pressed garlic
½ cup dry white wine
⅔ cup freshly grated parmesan cheese (about 3 ounces), preferably
    Parmigiano-Reggiano
Salt
Freshly ground black pepper
Freshly grated parmesan cheese, preferably Parmigiano-Reggiano, for serving

Place the rice in a bowl and add cold water to cover. Stir vigorously with your fingertips, then drain off the water. Repeat this procedure several times until the water runs almost clear. Drain well.

In a saucepan, bring the broth to a boil over high heat, then reduce the heat to low and keep the broth at a simmer while cooking the rice.

Heat 4 tablespoons of the butter in a heavy, deep sauté pan or skillet over medium-high heat. Add the onion and sauté until soft but not browned, about 5 minutes. Add the garlic and drained rice and sauté until all the grains of the rice are well coated, about 2 minutes. Stir in the wine and cook, stirring, until the wine has evaporated, about 3 minutes. Add ½ cup of the simmering broth, adjusting the heat under the rice if the liquid is evaporating too quickly. Keep the rice at a simmer and stir almost continuously, scraping the bottom and sides of the pan, until the liquid has been absorbed.

Continue to add the broth ½ cup at a time each time the rice becomes dry, and continue to stir the rice as it cooks. As the risotto approaches completion, add the broth only ¼ cup at a time. You may not need it all before the rice is done, or you may need more, in which case add hot water. Cook until the rice is tender but firm to the bite, about 25 minutes in all.

When the rice is done, add the remaining 1 tablespoon butter and the cheese and stir for about 2 minutes. Completed risotto should be creamy but not soupy; if it is too dry, add a little more broth. Season with salt and pepper to taste. Serve immediately. Pass additional parmesan cheese at the table.

Makes 6 servings.

Variations on page 56.

Variations on page 56.

Risotto al Parmigiano

Basic Risotto with Parmesan Cheese

*U*se this basic recipe as a guide for preparing the suggested variations or creating your own recipes with a host of optional additions. Most Italian recipe writers urge the use of a lightly flavored broth and abhor the use of canned broth; I enjoy stock with a bit more flavor and do not find canned substitutes objectionable.

Imported rice for making risotto is available in specialty-food markets and some well-stocked supermarkets. ❧

55

USING LEFTOVER RISOTTO

Form cold risotto into small cakes and pan-fry in unsalted butter until golden brown on both sides. Serve as a side dish.

Form cold risotto into small balls and poke a small cube of mozzarella into the center of each ball. Deep-fry in olive oil or vegetable oil until golden. Serve as an antipasto. 🐚

56

Basil Risotto (*Risotto al basilico*). Add a handful of fresh basil leaves to the broth when heating. Strain out the basil before using the liquid. Just before the risotto is done, chop or shred enough fresh basil to equal 1 cup and stir it into the rice along with the butter and cheese.

Beef Risotto (*Risotto al bistecca*). Use equal portions of beef broth and tomato juice for cooking the risotto. Season six 3-ounce boneless beef tenderloin steaks with salt and pepper to taste. Place each steak between 2 sheets of waxed paper or plastic wrap and pound with a mallet or other flat, heavy instrument to an even thickness of about ¼ inch. Sprinkle a fine layer of salt over the bottom of a heavy skillet and place over high heat. When the salt begins to brown and the pan is almost but not quite smoking, add the beef and sear on each side until well browned, then reduce the heat to medium-low, top each steak with about 1 tablespoon unsalted butter and cook, turning several times, until done to preference, about 6 minutes total for medium-rare. Remove the beef from the pan. Add about ¼ cup *each* beef broth and tomato juice to the pan, scraping up all browned-on bits, and cook over high heat until slightly reduced. Stir in 3 tablespoons chopped, drained sun-dried tomatoes packed in oil and 3 tablespoons coarsely chopped, pitted Italian-style ripe olives and heat through. Top each serving of rice with a steak, then pour the pan juices over the top.

Lamb Risotto (*Risotto al agnello*). Marinate boned lamb as described on page 86. Make the risotto, using broth made from lamb bones. Grill or roast boned lamb until done to preference, then slice into small pieces, catching all meat juices in a rimmed tray. Serve the lamb on top of the risotto and drizzle the accumulated lamb juices over the dish.

Saffron Risotto (*Risotto alla milanese*). Add ¼ teaspoon powdered saffron, or ½ teaspoon saffron threads, crushed, to ½ cup of the warm broth and set aside. Add the saffron-infused broth to the rice about halfway through the cooking.

Seafood Risotto (*Risotto al frutti di mare*). Substitute mildly flavored homemade fish stock or plain water for the broth. Cut mixed cooked shellfish and/or fish into small pieces to equal 2 cups. About 5 minutes before the rice is done, stir in the shellfish and/or fish and ½ cup peeled, seeded, and chopped ripe tomato. Omit the cheese.

Vegetable Risotto (*Risotto al verdura*). Substitute flavorful homemade or canned vegetable broth for the chicken or meat broth. Cut vegetables such as broccoli, carrots, or squash into small pieces to equal 2 cups. After cooking the onion and garlic, stir in the vegetables and cook until crisp-tender. Remove about half of the vegetables to a bowl and set aside. Add the drained rice to the pan and proceed as directed in the basic recipe. Stir in the reserved vegetables about 5 minutes before the rice is done. Alternatively, in a separate pot, cook tender vegetables such as asparagus or green peas until crisp-tender, then stir the drained vegetables into the rice about halfway through cooking.

RISOTTO DI POLLO
AFFUMICATO

SMOKED CHICKEN RISOTTO

*A*n excellent cold-weather dish and one that I often enjoy as a complete supper along with a salad. I order the smoked chicken in advance from my local purveyor of specialty foods and use the leftover meat the next day in a sandwich prepared with homemade or purchased focaccia (page 160). 🐦

58

1½ cups short-grain Italian rice such as Arborio, Carnaroli, or Vialone Nano
About 5 cups Italian-Style Broth (page 157), made from chicken, or 5 cups canned chicken broth, preferably reduced-sodium type
¼ teaspoon powdered saffron, or ½ teaspoon saffron threads, crushed, or to taste
5 tablespoons unsalted butter
½ cup minced shallot or red onion
1 cup chopped fresh mushrooms, preferably porcini, chanterelles, or similar flavorful varieties, coarsely chopped
1 teaspoon minced or pressed garlic
¼ cup chopped drained sun-dried tomatoes packed in olive oil
½ cup dry white wine
1¼ cups chopped or shredded smoked chicken
½ cup freshly grated parmesan cheese (about 2 ounces), preferably Parmigiano-Reggiano
Salt
Freshly ground black pepper
Freshly grated parmesan cheese, preferably Parmigiano-Reggiano, for serving

Place the rice in a bowl and add cold water to cover. Stir vigorously with your fingertips, then drain off the water. Repeat this procedure several times until the water runs almost clear. Drain well.

In a saucepan, bring the broth to a boil over high heat, then reduce the heat to low and keep the broth at a simmer while cooking the rice. Remove ½ cup of the stock and stir the saffron into it; reserve.

Heat 4 tablespoons of the butter in a heavy-bottomed, deep sauté pan or skillet over medium-high heat. Add the shallot or onion and mushrooms and sauté until the onion is lightly golden and the mushrooms are tender, about 5 minutes. Add the garlic, sun-dried tomatoes, and drained rice and sauté until all the grains of the rice are well coated, about 2 minutes. Stir in the wine and cook, stirring, until the wine has evaporated, about 3 minutes. Add ½ cup of the simmering broth, adjusting the heat under the rice if the liquid is evaporating too quickly. Keep the rice at a simmer and stir almost continuously, scraping the bottom and sides of the pan, until the liquid has been absorbed.

Continue to add the broth ½ cup at a time each time the rice becomes dry, and continue to stir the rice as it cooks. Use the saffron-infused broth after the first 15 minutes of cooking. As the risotto approaches completion, add the broth only ¼ cup at a time. You may not need it all before the rice is done, or you may need more, in which case add hot water. Cook until the rice is tender but firm to the bite, about 25 minutes in all. When properly cooked, the rice should be creamy but not soupy.

About 5 minutes before you think the rice will be done, stir in the smoked chicken to heat through. When the rice is done, stir in the remaining 1 tablespoon butter and the cheese. Season to taste with salt and pepper. Serve immediately. Pass parmesan cheese at the table.

Makes 6 servings.

LOBSTER RISOTTO

LOBSTER AND BROTH
2 gallons water
2 celery stalks, chopped
1 yellow onion, quartered
3 or 4 fresh parsley sprigs, preferably flat-leaf type
2 bay leaves
3 live Maine lobsters (about 1 pound each)
¼ cup (½ stick) unsalted butter
2 cups chopped leek
2 cups chopped celery
2 cups chopped peeled carrot
1½ cups chopped ripe or drained canned tomato
¾ cup chopped red sweet pepper
1½ cups dry white wine
Salt

1½ cups short-grain Italian rice such as Arborio, Carnaroli, or Vialone Nano
¼ cup (½ stick) unsalted butter
½ cup chopped leek
1½ cups dry white wine
1 cup freshly shelled, young, tender peas, cooked until crisp-tender,
  or thawed frozen peas
Salt
Freshly ground black pepper
Slivered leek, including some of the tender green portion, for garnish
Ripe cherry tomatoes, preferably yellow varieties, sliced in half, for garnish

To cook the lobster, combine the water, chopped celery stalks, onion, parsley, and bay leaves in a large pot and bring to a boil over high heat. Drop 1 lobster head-first into the boiling water and cook until the shell turns bright red and the meat is opaque, about 12 minutes. Lift out the lobster, drain well, and set aside to cool. Return the water to a boil and cook the remaining lobsters, one at a time, in the same manner. Reserve the cooking liquid.

When the lobsters are cool enough to handle, break the tail off from each body. Using scissors, cut a lengthwise slit along the soft underpart of the tail, then remove and set aside the meat and shell; discard the vein that runs along the back. Crack the claws and remove and set aside the meat and shell. Rinse away the contents of the lobster body and set the shell and legs aside. Slice the lobster meat into bite-sized pieces, cover tightly, and refrigerate. Coarsely chop the lobster shell pieces and set aside.

Recipe continues on page 62.

RISOTTO DI ARAGOSTA
LOBSTER RISOTTO

*S*hrimp or crawfish could be used in place of the lobster. For a fancy presentation, reserve the lobster claws intact and use them and the tail fans to garnish the dish. ❧

To make the lobster broth, melt the butter in a large saucepan over medium heat. Add the chopped leek, celery, and carrot and sauté until the vegetables are soft, about 5 minutes. Add the reserved lobster shells and sauté for about 4 minutes longer. Stir in the tomato, sweet pepper, wine, and 8 cups of the reserved cooking liquid. Bring to a boil, then reduce the heat to low and simmer for 20 minutes. Strain through a fine-mesh sieve lined with dampened cheesecloth into a clean saucepan and return to a boil over medium-high heat. Using a wire skimmer or slotted utensil, skim off and discard any scum that rises to the surface. Cook until the liquid is reduced by half. Season to taste with salt. Reduce the heat to low and keep the broth at a simmer while cooking the rice.

Now begin to prepare the rice. Place the rice in a bowl and add cold water to cover. Stir vigorously with your fingertips, then drain off the water. Repeat this procedure several times until the water runs almost clear. Drain well.

Heat the butter in a heavy, deep sauté pan or skillet over medium-high heat. Add the chopped leek and sauté until lightly golden, about 5 minutes. Add the drained rice and sauté until all the grains of the rice are well coated, about 2 minutes. Stir in the wine and cook, stirring, until the wine has evaporated, about 3 minutes. Add ½ cup of the simmering broth, adjusting the heat under the rice if the broth is evaporating too quickly. Keep the rice at a simmer and stir almost continuously, scraping the bottom and sides of the pan, until the liquid has been absorbed.

Continue to add the broth ½ cup at a time each time the rice becomes dry, and continue to stir the rice as it cooks. As the risotto approaches completion, add the broth only ¼ cup at a time. You may not need it all before the rice is done, or you may need more, in which case add hot water. Cook until the rice is tender but firm to the bite, about 25 minutes in all. When properly cooked, the rice should be creamy but not soupy.

About 5 minutes before you think the rice will be done, stir in the reserved lobster meat and peas to heat through. Season to taste with salt and pepper. Spoon into shallow bowls, garnish with the slivered leek and cherry tomatoes and serve immediately.

Makes 6 servings.

SPINACH DUMPLINGS IN GORGONZOLA SAUCE

SPINACH DUMPLINGS
8 ounces spinach
¾ cup ricotta cheese (about 6 ounces), drained
½ cup unseasoned dried bread crumbs
1 egg, beaten
¼ cup freshly grated parmesan cheese (about 1 ounce), preferably
  Parmigiano-Reggiano
2 tablespoons finely chopped green onion, including tender
  green portion
¼ teaspoon salt
⅛ teaspoon freshly grated nutmeg
All-purpose flour for dusting

GORGONZOLA SAUCE
1 cup heavy (whipping) cream
1 cup crumbled creamy Gorgonzola cheese (about 5 ounces)
Salt
Freshly ground black pepper
Freshly grated Parmigiano-Reggiano for serving

FOR GRATIN (OPTIONAL)
Softened unsalted butter for greasing baking dishes
3 tablespoons unseasoned dried bread crumbs
2 tablespoons freshly grated parmesan cheese, preferably Parmigiano-Reggiano

To make the dumplings, wash the spinach carefully to remove any sand or grit
and discard any tough stems. Place the damp spinach in a sauté pan or heavy
skillet and cook over high heat, stirring frequently, until the spinach wilts and turns
bright green, about 5 minutes. Drain in a colander and squeeze out as much liquid
as possible. Transfer to a food processor fitted with a metal blade and chop finely.
Alternatively, finely chop the spinach with a sharp knife and transfer to a bowl.

Add the ricotta cheese, bread crumbs, egg, parmesan cheese, onion, salt, and
nutmeg to the spinach and blend thoroughly. Cover tightly and refrigerate for
about 2 hours.

Using about 2 teaspoons to form each dumpling, roll the spinach mixture between
your palms to form balls. Roll the balls lightly in flour to dust them on all sides,
then arrange them on a tray lined with waxed paper. Cover and refrigerate for
about 30 minutes.

To make the sauce, in a heavy-bottomed saucepan, combine the cream and
Gorgonzola. Place over medium heat and bring to a boil, stirring frequently.
Reduce the heat to low and stir until slightly thickened, about 5 minutes. Season

Recipe continues on page 64.

*S*erve these cloud-light dumplings

with the rich sauce or place the

combination in gratin pans and bake

until the top is crusty. Thawed

frozen spinach may be substituted for

the cooked fresh spinach; be sure to

squeeze out as much liquid as

possible. Potato gnocchi may be

used in place of the spinach

dumplings; see my Potato

Cookbook for a recipe. ❧

63

to taste with salt and pepper, and continue to stir until smooth, about 2 minutes longer. Keep warm.

In a large pot, bring several quarts of water to a simmer. Drop the dumplings, a few at a time, into the simmering water; do not crowd the pan. Regulate the heat so that the water remains at a simmer and cook until the dumplings pop up to the surface, about 2 minutes. Cook for about 2 minutes longer. Using a slotted utensil, remove the dumplings to a tray lined with paper toweling to drain well. Cook the remaining dumplings in the same manner.

Divide the sauce evenly among 4 individual warmed plates or bowls. Arrange the dumplings over the sauce, sprinkle the parmesan cheese over the top, and serve immediately.

Alternatively, to serve as a gratin, preheat an oven to 350°F. Grease 4 individual flameproof gratin dishes or other shallow baking dishes with softened butter. Divide about half of the sauce evenly among the dishes. Arrange the dumplings over the sauce, then spoon the remaining sauce over the dumplings. Bake for 10 minutes.

Meanwhile, preheat a broiler.

Remove the gratins from the oven. Sprinkle with the bread crumbs and parmesan cheese. Place under the preheated broiler until the cheese melts and a light crust forms, 2 to 3 minutes. Serve immediately.

Makes 4 servings.

Baked Dumplings, Roman Style

5 cups milk
1½ teaspoons salt, or to taste
½ teaspoon freshly ground black pepper, or to taste
⅛ teaspoon freshly grated nutmeg, or to taste
1½ cups coarsely ground semolina flour, preferably imported
   from Italy
1 cup freshly grated parmesan cheese (about 4 ounces), preferably
   Parmigiano-Reggiano
3 egg yolks, lightly beaten
3 tablespoons minced fresh sage, or 1 tablespoon crumbled dried sage
4 tablespoons (½ stick) unsalted butter, melted
Softened unsalted butter for greasing baking sheet and dish and dotting top

In a heavy-bottomed saucepan, combine the milk, salt, pepper, and nutmeg over medium heat. Bring the milk almost to a boil. Reduce the heat to the lowest possible position and gradually pour in the semolina in a thin, steady stream, stirring constantly with a wooden spoon or wire whisk. The mixture will thicken quickly, but continue cooking and stirring, scraping the bottom of the pan, until the mixture forms a very thick mass that pulls away from the sides of the pan, about 15 minutes. Remove from the heat.

Quickly stir ¾ cup of the parmesan cheese, the egg yolks, sage, and 2 tablespoons of the melted butter into the hot semolina mixture. mixing well.

Grease a large shallow baking sheet with softened butter. Using a metal spatula dipped in cold water from time to time, spread the thick mixture into a layer about ¼ inch thick. Let cool to room temperature, then cover and refrigerate until the mixture is cold and firm, about 1 hour.

Preheat an oven to 400°F. Grease a 9-by-13-inch baking dish with softened butter; set aside.

Using a biscuit cutter or straight-sided glass 1½ to 2 inches in diameter, cut the semolina sheet into rounds, dipping the cutter into cold water between cuts. Place the dumplings in the prepared baking dish, arranging them in slightly overlapping rows to form a single layer. Dot with softened butter and sprinkle with the remaining ¼ cup parmesan cheese.

Bake until golden and crusty, about 20 minutes. Remove from the oven and let stand about 5 minutes before serving directly from the baking dish.

Makes 6 to 8 servings.

Gnocchi alla Romana
Baked Dumplings, Roman Style

Unlike most Italian first courses, this dish can be prepared a day or two ahead and refrigerated, then baked at the last minute. Semolina is ground from hard durum wheat; look for it in specialty food stores, Italian markets, and some supermarkets.

To serve two or three, cut only enough circles from the chilled semolina mixture to fill individual ramekins or a small bake-and-serve dish. Reserve the remaining semolina for another baking up to 3 days later. Or use all of the semolina to fill small dishes and freeze for up to 2 months before baking. ☙

POLENTINA CON FORMAGGIO

CREAMY POLENTA WITH CHEESE

When cornmeal mush is cooked to a soft, spoonable consistency, the Italians call it polentina *to differentiate from the firmer polenta that can be cut into sections. Finely ground yellow or white cornmeal is favored in the Veneto; the coarse yellow meal sold in America as polenta is preferred in Piedmont and Lombardy.* 🐌

CREAMY POLENTA WITH CHEESE

2 cups cornmeal (see recipe introduction)
1 tablespoon salt, or to taste
10 cups Italian-Style Broth (page 157), made from meat and chicken;
    6 cups canned chicken or vegetable broth, preferably reduced-sodium type, diluted with 4 cups water; or 10 cups water
About 2 cups *mascarpone*, Gorgonzola, or other soft creamy cheese, or freshly grated Parmigiano-Reggiano

In a heavy saucepan or copper polenta pan, combine the cornmeal, salt, and broth or water; stir well. Place over medium-high heat and bring to a simmer, stirring occasionally with a wooden spoon. Reduce the heat to low and simmer, stirring frequently and scraping the bottom of the pot with the spoon, until the mixture thickens to the texture of cream of wheat, about 30 minutes; add more liquid if necessary to achieve a smooth, soft consistency.

Pour into large, shallow individual warmed bowls and top with the cheese of choice.

Makes 6 servings.

VARIATIONS

Herbed Creamy Polenta (*Polentina d'erbe*). Stir 3 tablespoons minced fresh basil, oregano, sage, or rosemary into the polentina about 5 minutes before it is ready. Use Gorgonzola or Parmigiano-Reggiano cheese.

Red Pepper Creamy Polenta (*Polentina di peperoni*). Roast, peel, and seed 2 red sweet peppers as directed on page 152. Place in a food processor fitted with a metal blade or in a blender and purée. Stir into the saucepan with the cornmeal and other ingredients at the beginning of cooking.

POLENTA ARROSTA CON SALSA DI BALSAMICO E FUNGHI

ROASTED POLENTA WITH BALSAMIC SAUCE AND MUSHROOMS

The idea for this dish came from a more complex version served at Tra Vigne, a Tuscan-style restaurant near my home in the Napa Valley. I created this simpler variation for home cooks. 🖋

Polenta (page 158), with additions of butter and parmesan cheese
Balsamic Sauce (page 156)
Olive oil for brushing on polenta slices
3 tablespoons unsalted butter
8 ounces fresh mushrooms, preferably porcini, shiitakes, or other flavorful varieties, sliced or chopped
Fresh bay leaves for garnish (optional)

The day before serving, prepare the polenta as directed. Pour into a greased 5-by-9-inch loaf pan, cover tightly, and refrigerate until firm.

Make the Balsamic Sauce. Set aside.

Preheat an oven to 450°F.

Turn the chilled polenta out of the pan onto a cutting surface. Cut the polenta into slices about ¾ inch thick, then cut into desired shapes. Lightly brush on all sides with olive oil and place on a baking sheet. Roast in the oven until crisp and golden on the bottom, about 10 minutes. Turn and roast until golden on the other side, 5 to 10 minutes longer.

Meanwhile, in a heavy-bottomed sauté pan or skillet, melt the butter over medium-high heat. Add the mushrooms and sauté for about 2 minutes. Reduce the heat to medium-low and cook until tender, about 8 minutes longer, depending upon the variety. Set aside and keep warm.

To serve, gently reheat the Balsamic Sauce and ladle a pool of it onto individual plates. Top with the polenta slices. Spoon the mushrooms onto the polenta and drizzle a bit more of the sauce over the mushrooms. Garnish with bay leaves (if used) and serve immediately.

Makes 8 servings.

BAKED POLENTA CASSEROLE

Polenta (page 158), made with 12 cups liquid and 3 cups cornmeal and
  with additions of ½ cup (1 stick) unsalted butter and 1 cup freshly
  grated parmesan cheese
Tomato Sauce (page 155)
1 cup pine nuts
Softened unsalted butter for greasing baking dish
2 cups freshly shredded Italian Fontina cheese (about 10 ounces)
2 cups crumbled creamy sweet Gorgonzola cheese (about 8 ounces)
1 cup freshly grated parmesan cheese (about 4 ounces), preferably
  Parmigiano-Reggiano
Chopped or shredded fresh basil or parsley, preferably flat-leaf type,
  for sprinkling

The day before serving, prepare the polenta as directed and divide it among
3 greased 9-by-13-inch baking pans or into 2 greased 5-by-9-inch loaf pans, cover
tightly, and refrigerate.

Prepare the Tomato Sauce; set aside.

In a small, heavy skillet, place the pine nuts over medium heat. Toast, shaking
the pan or stirring frequently, until the nuts are lightly golden and fragrant, about
5 minutes. Pour onto a plate to cool.

Preheat an oven to 350°F. If using polenta chilled in loaf pans, grease a round
3-quart baking dish or a 9-by-13-inch baking pan.

If the polenta was chilled in 9-by-13-inch pans, turn the polenta from 2 of the pans
onto a work surface; leave 1 sheet in its pan to serve as the bottom layer of the
casserole. If the polenta was chilled in loaf pans, turn it out onto a work surface,
cut it into slices about ½ inch thick, and arrange an even layer of the slices in the
prepared pan, cutting slices as necessary to fill any holes. Scatter half of the Fontina
and Gorgonzola cheeses in an even layer over the polenta and sprinkle with about
one third of the toasted pine nuts. Top with another layer of polenta and then with
the remaining Fontina and Gorgonzola and half of the remaining pine nuts. Cover
with a final layer of polenta. Sprinkle the parmesan cheese and remaining pine nuts
evenly over the top.

Bake until the cheeses melt and the dish is heated through, about 1 hour. Set aside
to cool slightly while reheating the Tomato Sauce.

To serve, ladle some of the hot Tomato Sauce onto each individual plate. Cut the
polenta casserole into squares or wedges and place on top of the sauce. Sprinkle
each serving with basil or parsley and serve immediately.

Makes 6 to 8 servings.

POLENTA PASTICCIATA
BAKED POLENTA CASSEROLE

*Vary this meatless dish by
substituting a favorite meat sauce.
Or fill the pie with sautéed
mushrooms, a combination of other
cheeses, cooked spinach or other
vegetables, or other favorite lasagna
fillings.* ❧

SECOND COURSES

(*Secondi piatti*)

—

SIDE DISHES

(*Contorni*)

—

SALADS

(*Insalate*)

*I*n Italy, second courses, or *secondi piatti*, usually of fish, poultry, or meat, are

not thought of as main courses as they are in America. They are considered dishes of

equal importance to what precedes and follows.

Although they are called side dishes, or *contorni*, vegetables are actually a course

of their own. They may follow the second course or be served alongside of it. Sometimes

green or vegetable salads (*insalate*) take the place of cooked vegetables, whereas meat,

poultry, or fish salads are always served as *antipasti* or as light meals.

In some of the second-course recipes that follow, I've suggested ways of preparing

accompanying vegetables in the recipe introductions where full-scale recipes seem

unnecessary. Rounding out this section are a few of my favorite vegetable preparations

and a handful of salads.

PESCE ALLA GRIGLIA
GRILLED FISH

One of the best fish feasts that I can recall was underneath the canvas overhang of Delfino, a popular restaurant only a few feet from the deep blue sea in Portofino on the Italian Riviera. Barbara, our perky waitress, made an order of grilled fresh fish sound irresistible, which it proved to be. It was a huge tray topped with a sizzling-hot stone slab overlaid with lettuce leaves framing an artful array of charred fish, shellfish, and vegetables. It is easy to re-create such a feast at home relying upon whatever harvests of the sea are available fresh. ❦

GRILLED FISH

Before grilling the fish, brush assorted small or sliced larger vegetables with olive oil and grill until tender; keep the vegetables warm while you cook the fish. If you wish to add shellfish, prepare and cook them in the same manner.

2 pounds firm-fleshed fish steaks or fillets, ½ to ¾ inch thick
Salt
Freshly ground black pepper
2 teaspoons minced fresh oregano, or 1 teaspoon crumbled dried oregano
¼ cup olive oil, preferably extra-virgin
2 tablespoons freshly squeezed lemon juice
Vegetable oil for brushing on grill rack
Fresh fig leaves or grape leaves (optional)
Lemon wedges for serving

Quickly rinse the fish under running cold water and pat dry with paper toweling. Sprinkle all over with salt and pepper and place in a large shallow bowl. Sprinkle with the oregano. Pour the olive oil and lemon juice over the fish and turn each piece several times to coat thoroughly. Cover and marinate at room temperature for about 1 hour, turning several times.

Prepare an open grill for hot direct-heat cooking. Position the grill rack 4 to 5 inches above the heat source.

When the fire is ready, lightly brush the grill rack or the inside of a hinged wire basket with vegetable oil. Place the fish on the grill rack or in the hinged wire basket directly over heat; reserve marinade for basting. Cook, turning once, until the thickest portion of flesh is just opaque when tested by cutting with a small, sharp knife, about 5 to 6 minutes total. Brush the fish with the marinade from time to time while cooking.

Line a platter or individual plates with leaves (if used) and arrange the fish on top. Accompany with lemon wedges for squeezing over the fish.

Makes 4 servings.

MIXED FRIED SEAFOOD WITH MUSTARD SAUCE

MUSTARD SAUCE
¼ cup whole-grain mustard
¼ cup extra-virgin olive oil
2 tablespoons freshly squeezed lemon juice
1 tablespoon sugar
Salt
Freshly ground black pepper

12 ounces medium-sized shrimp, peeled and deveined
12 ounces bay scallops
1 pound small squid, cleaned and cut into ½-inch rings, with tentacles reserved
Salt
Canola oil or other high-quality vegetable oil for deep-fat frying
About ¾ cup Italian rice flour or all-purpose flour
Lemon wedges for serving

To make the Mustard Sauce, in a bowl, combine the mustard, oil, lemon juice, sugar, and salt and pepper to taste. Stir to mix well and set aside.

Quickly rinse the shellfish under running cold water and pat dry with paper toweling. Sprinkle lightly with salt and set aside.

In a deep-fat fryer or a deep saucepan, pour in the oil to a depth of about 2 inches. Heat to 375°F, or until a small piece of bread dropped into the hot oil turns golden brown within a few seconds. Meanwhile, preheat an oven to 200°F. Line a baking sheet with several thicknesses of paper toweling. Spread about one fourth of the Mustard Sauce on each of 4 individual plates.

Place the shrimp in a colander set over a bowl. Sprinkle with about ¼ cup of the flour, tossing the shrimp lightly to coat them evenly with the flour. Shake the colander to remove excess flour.

When the oil is hot, place some of the shrimp into a wire basket or slotted spoon and carefully lower into the oil. Avoid overcrowding the pan. Cook, stirring frequently, until golden on all sides, 1 to 2 minutes, depending upon size. Transfer to the paper towel–lined tray to drain; place in the oven to keep warm.

Flour and fry the scallops in the same way, cooking for 1 to 2 minutes, depending upon size. Transfer to the warming tray.

Flour and fry the squid in the same way, cooking for only about 1 minute (overcooking will toughen squid). Drain briefly on paper toweling.

Quickly arrange the shrimp, scallops, and squid over the sauce on the plates. Serve piping hot. Offer lemon wedges for squeezing over the shellfish.

Makes 4 servings.

FRITTO MISTO DI FRUTTI DI MARE CON SALSA DI MOSTARDO

MIXED FRIED SEAFOOD
WITH MUSTARD SAUCE

*I*nstead of a mixture, only one type of shellfish may be used. This dish may also be offered as an informal appetizer for six or more by placing it on a platter in the middle of the table for sharing.

The non-Italian mustard sauce offers a tangy accent. To lighten the dish, toss some bitter greens such as curly endive with some of the sauce and top with the seafood. In lieu of the sauce, serve the mixed fry with lemon wedges for squeezing over the top. ❧

CHICKEN CUTLETS WITH PROSCIUTTO AND SAGE

SALTIMBOCCA DI POLLO ALLA ROMANA

CHICKEN CUTLETS WITH PROSCIUTTO AND SAGE

*T*oday many of my friends avoid eating veal, so here's a version of this Roman favorite made with chicken breasts. When serving veal fanciers, you may choose to substitute about 1 pound thinly sliced veal for the chicken breasts. Saltimbocca translates to "jump in the mouth." ❧

80

4 boned and skinned chicken breast halves
Salt
Freshly ground black pepper
3 ounces thinly sliced prosciutto
8 whole fresh sage leaves
About 4 tablespoons (½ stick) unsalted butter
About 2 tablespoons olive oil
1 cup dry white wine

Quickly rinse the chicken breasts under cold running water and pat dry with paper toweling. Discard the tendons and any connective tissue or fat from the breasts, then separate the little fillet from each breast and reserve for another purpose. Place each breast between 2 sheets of waxed paper or plastic wrap and pound with a mallet or other flat, heavy instrument to a uniform thickness of about ⅛ inch. Lightly sprinkle the chicken with salt and pepper.

Trim the prosciutto slices to fit atop the chicken slices precisely. Top each chicken piece with a slice of prosciutto and 1 or 2 sage leaves, securing each leaf in place with a toothpick.

In a heavy-bottomed sauté pan or skillet (without a nonstick coating), combine 2 tablespoons butter and 2 tablespoons olive oil over medium-high heat. When the butter stops foaming, add as many of the chicken pieces as will fit comfortably without crowding the pan. Brown on one side, then turn and cook on the other side until browned and opaque all the way through, 4 to 5 minutes total; use a small sharp knife to check for doneness. Remove the chicken to a warmed platter and cover to keep warm. Cook the remaining chicken in the same way, adding a little more butter and oil if necessary to prevent sticking.

When all of the chicken is cooked, discard the cooking fat from the pan. Return the pan to medium-high heat. Add the white wine and salt and pepper to taste to the pan and scrape the bottom of the pan with a wooden utensil to loosen any browned bits. Reduce the wine to about ½ cup, then add the remaining 2 tablespoons butter and stir until melted. Discard the toothpicks from the chicken and transfer the slices to 4 individual plates. Pour the pan sauce over the chicken and serve immediately.

Makes 4 servings.

SAUTÉED RABBIT AND VEGETABLES

*CONIGLIO E VERDURE
ALLA PADELLA*

SAUTÉED RABBIT
AND VEGETABLES

*O*ne spectacular day in May, I
enjoyed a preparation similar to this
one underneath a wisteria canopy at
the Hotel Florence ristorante perched
on the banks of Lake Como. I liked
the idea that the rabbit was already
cut into small bites. Be sure to cut
the vegetables into the same-sized
matchstick pieces. ❧

MARINADE
1 cup dry white wine
¼ cup red wine vinegar
3 garlic cloves, unpeeled, crushed
3 or 4 fresh rosemary sprigs
4 or 5 fresh parsley sprigs, preferably flat-leaf type
1 bay leaf
½ teaspoon whole black peppercorns

2 young rabbits (5½ to 6 pounds total weight), meat removed from
    bones and cut into bite-sized pieces
4 tablespoons (½ stick) unsalted butter
4 tablespoons olive oil
3 cups julienned red onion
3 cups julienned carrot
3 cups julienned zucchini
Salt
Freshly ground black pepper
2 tablespoons sugar, or to taste
Minced fresh parsley, preferably flat-leaf type, for garnish

In a nonreactive container, combine the marinade ingredients. Add the rabbit meat,
toss to coat well, cover tightly, and refrigerate, stirring several times, for at least 6
hours or for as long as 24 hours.

Strain the rabbit marinade through a sieve into a bowl and reserve. Discard the garlic
and herbs. Pat the meat dry with paper toweling and sprinkle lightly with salt.

In a heavy-bottomed sauté pan or skillet, heat 3 tablespoons of the butter and
3 tablespoons of the olive oil over medium heat. When the butter stops foaming,
add the onion, carrot, and zucchini and sauté until crisp-tender, 3 to 4 minutes.
Season with salt and pepper to taste. Using a slotted utensil, transfer the vegetables
to a bowl and cover to keep warm.

To the pan in which the vegetables were cooked, add the remaining 1 tablespoon
each butter and olive oil over medium heat. When the butter stops foaming, add the
rabbit and sauté until the meat is tender when pierced with a fork or small, sharp
knife, 6 to 8 minutes. Remove to a separate bowl.

To the pan in which the rabbit was cooked, add the strained marinade, increase the
heat to high, and scrape the pan bottom to loosen any browned bits. Stir in the sugar
and boil rapidly until the liquid thickens slightly. Taste and add salt and pepper if
needed. Return the rabbit to the pan to heat through, about 2 minutes.

To serve, spoon a bed of the vegetables onto each individual plate. Top with the
rabbit and then the pan sauce. Sprinkle with parsley and serve immediately.

Makes 6 servings.

PORK STEW

3 pounds boneless pork, cut into 1-inch cubes
2 tablespoons all-purpose flour, preferably unbleached
¼ cup olive oil, or more if needed
4 ounces Italian bacon (*pancetta*), chopped
2 cups chopped red onion
1 teaspoon minced or pressed garlic
1 cup dry red wine
1 cup Italian-Style Broth (page 157), made from meat or chicken, or
  canned beef or chicken broth, preferably reduced-sodium type
5 cups peeled, seeded, drained, and chopped ripe or canned plum tomato
2 tablespoons tomato paste
1 tablespoon minced fresh sage, or 1½ teaspoons crumbled dried sage
1 tablespoon minced fresh rosemary, or 1½ teaspoons crumbled dried rosemary
Salt
Freshly ground black pepper
1 cup pitted Italian-style black olives, drained

GREMOLADA
3 tablespoons minced fresh parsley, preferably flat-leaf type
1 teaspoon minced or pressed garlic
1 tablespoon minced or grated fresh lemon zest

Quickly rinse the pork under running cold water and pat dry with paper toweling. Place the meat in a colander set over a bowl. Sprinkle with the flour, turning the meat to coat lightly and evenly with the flour. Shake the colander to remove excess flour.

In a heavy stew pot such as a dutch oven, heat the olive oil over medium-high heat. Add as many of the pork pieces as will fit comfortably without crowding the pot and brown on all sides. Using a slotted utensil or tongs, transfer the browned pork to a plate. Brown the remaining pork in the same manner, adding more oil as necessary to prevent sticking.

Add the *pancetta* and onion to the same pot in which the pork was browned reduce the heat to medium and cook, stirring frequently, until the onion is golden, about 10 minutes. Add the garlic and cook for 1 minute longer. Stir in the wine and broth and scrape up any browned bits on the pan bottom. Return the pork to the pot, lower the heat and simmer until the liquid has reduced by half, about 20 minutes.

Stir in the tomato, tomato paste, sage, rosemary, and salt and pepper to taste. Reduce the heat to low, cover tightly, and simmer, stirring occasionally, until the meat is tender, 1 to 1½ hours. About 30 minutes before the stew is done, stir in the olives.

A few minutes before serving, make the *gremolada* by combining all the ingredients in a bowl.

To serve, ladle the stew into bowls or onto plates, sprinkle with the *gremolada*, and serve immediately.

Makes 6 to 8 servings.

STUFATO DI MAIALE
PORK STEW

This recipe is based on a wild boar stew that I relished on a recent trip to Florence. Since most of us don't have access to wild boar, I've substituted pork. Beef, lamb or veal shanks, oxtails, or venison could also be used.

For a delectable combination, prepare Creamy Polenta (page 68), without the cheese, spoon it into shallow bowls or rimmed plates, and ladle the stew over the top.

COSTOLETTE D'AGNELLO
A SCOTTADITO

GRILLED LAMB CHOPS

Serve this Roman specialty with cooked young asparagus tossed in melted butter and sprinkled with freshly grated parmesan cheese, preferably Parmigiano-Reggiano. The little chops are traditionally eaten by holding the bone between the fingers. ❦

12 small lamb chops, cut from rack of young spring lamb
1 cup olive oil
½ cup freshly squeezed lemon juice
2 tablespoons chopped garlic
2 tablespoons chopped fresh rosemary
Salt
Freshly ground black pepper
Vegetable oil for brushing on grill rack
Lemon wedges for serving

Quickly rinse the lamb chops under cold running water and pat dry with paper toweling. Place in a shallow nonreactive container. Pour the oil and lemon juice over the lamb and sprinkle with the garlic and rosemary. Cover and marinate at room temperature for about 1 hour.

Prepare an open grill for moderate direct-heat cooking.

Remove the lamb and pat dry with paper toweling. Sprinkle with salt and pepper to taste.

When the fire is ready, lightly brush the grill rack with vegetable oil. Place the lamb chops on the rack and cook, turning once, until done to preference, about 3 minutes on each side for medium-rare.

Serve with lemon wedges for squeezing over the lamb.

Serves 4 to 6.

ABBACCHIO AL CACCIATORE

POT-ROASTED YOUNG LAMB

*I*taIian chefs and home cooks roast suckling lambs to welcome early spring. In America, however, the youngest butchered spring lamb is somewhat older. Any spring lamb, though, can be pot roasted, or braised, to produce a tender, succulent dish similar to American pot roast.

Serve the lamb with roasted whole potatoes, or with a rich gratin of salted and peppered potato slices layered in a baking dish with shredded Taleggio or Fontina cheese, drizzled with cream, and baked until tender and golden on top. ❧

88

5- to 6-pound leg of young lamb (weighed with bone in), boned,
   rolled, and tied
Salt
Freshly ground black pepper
3 tablespoons unsalted butter
3 tablespoons vegetable oil
10 garlic cloves, crushed
1 tablespoon minced fresh rosemary, or 1½ teaspoons
   crumbled dried rosemary
1 tablespoon minced fresh sage, or 1½ teaspoons crumbled dried sage
¾ cup dry white wine
Italian-Style Broth (page 157), made from lamb; canned chicken broth,
   preferably reduced-sodium type; or water, as needed
2 tablespoons dry white wine

Quickly rinse the lamb under cold running water and pat dry with paper toweling. Sprinkle with salt and pepper. In a heavy pot such as a dutch oven, combine the butter and oil over medium-high heat. When the butter stops foaming, add the lamb and brown well on all sides. Add the garlic, rosemary, sage, and the ¾ cup wine. Bring the wine to a boil, then reduce the heat to low, cover, and simmer, turning occasionally, until the lamb is very tender when pierced with a fork, about 3 hours. Add a little water if the pan becomes dry during cooking.

Transfer the lamb to a cutting surface and cover loosely with aluminum foil to keep warm.

Spoon off as much of the fat as possible from the cooking liquid in the pot. If there is considerable cooking liquid remaining, place over high heat and reduce to about 1 cup; if there is only a little cooking liquid, add broth or water to equal about 1 cup. Stir in the 2 tablespoons wine, increase the heat to high, and scrape up any browned bits from the pan bottom. In either case, strain the juices.

To serve, snip off and discard the string from the lamb and slice about ¼ inch thick. Arrange on a warmed platter or individual plates. Pour the hot pan juices over the lamb and serve at once.

Makes 6 servings.

COTOLETTE ALLA MILANESE

BREADED VEAL CUTLETS, MILANESE STYLE

*S*urrounded by a chorus of caged songbirds at Giannino in Milan, I feasted on these succulent chops. The veal was served with fried baskets made of shoestring potatoes, which were filled with small rounds of potato formed with a melon baller and then fried in a combination of rosemary-flavored butter and oil. See my Potato Cookbook *for directions on making potato baskets.* ❦

90

4 single-rib veal chops with bones intact, sliced about ¾ inch thick
Salt
2 eggs
About 2 cups fine fresh bread crumbs, from Italian or French bread
3 tablespoons unsalted butter
2 tablespoons vegetable oil

Quickly rinse the veal chops under running cold water and pat dry with paper toweling. Using a sharp knife, trim off the meat from the narrow end of each bone, leaving the exposed bone very clean. Using a meat cleaver, cut off the thick corner end bone from each chop. Cut away all fat, sinew, and membrane from the edges of the chops. Place the meat portion of each chop between 2 sheets of plastic wrap and pound with a flat, heavy mallet or other instrument until the veal is about half its original thickness. Lightly sprinkle the veal with salt.

In a shallow bowl, lightly beat the eggs.

Dip each veal chop into the beaten egg, shaking off the excess egg. Working over a plate, sprinkle one side of each chop with bread crumbs, then lay, breaded side down, on a plate. Sprinkle the other side with crumbs, lightly pressing on the crumbs with your fingertips so they adhere to the meat. Sprinkle both sides of the chops once again with crumbs, pressing to adhere. Set aside.

In a heavy sauté pan or skillet, combine the butter and oil over medium heat. As soon as the butter stops foaming, add the veal chops and cook, turning once, until golden brown on both sides, about 4 minutes on each side; the meat should be slightly pink inside. Serve immediately.

Serves 4.

GRILLED STEAK, FLORENTINE STYLE

1 steak, about 3 pounds and 3 inches thick (see recipe introduction)
Cracked black peppercorns
Kosher salt or coarse sea salt
Vegetable oil for brushing on grill rack
Extra-virgin olive oil for serving
Lemon wedges for serving

Prepare an open grill for moderate direct-heat cooking. Position the grill rack 4 to 5 inches above the heat source.

Quickly rinse the steak under cold running water and pat dry with paper toweling. Rub a generous amount of pepper into both sides of the steak and then sprinkle with salt.

When the flames have died and the coals are covered with ash, brush the grill rack with vegetable oil. Place the steak on the rack and cook until charred on one side, about 5 minutes. Using a spatula or tongs, turn and cook the second side until charred, about 4 minutes longer. Continue cooking, turning a couple of more times, until the outside is well charred yet the meat is still rare when cut into with a small, sharp knife, about 5 minutes longer.

Remove the steak to a plate on which it can be cut. At the table cut the steak into 4 pieces, giving portions of the fillet and contrafillet sides to each person. Offer olive oil and lemon wedges for seasoning to each person's preference.

Makes 4 servings.

BISTECCA ALLA FIORENTINA

GRILLED STEAK,
FLORENTINE STYLE

Here is Italian cookery at its simplest and tastiest, but only if high-quality beef is selected. Purchase the tenderest beef you can find in order to approximate the buttery yet lean Tuscan counterpart. Ask your butcher for a steak that contains both fillet and contrafillet sections, usually called Porterhouse.

I like to serve a mixed green salad (made in the same way as the Fresh Herb Salad on page 110) alongside such a meaty feast. ❦

93

BRACIOLE PIZZAIOLA

PANFRIED BEEF IN
SPICY TOMATO SAUCE

Chicken or turkey breast, pork loin,
or veal scallops may be substituted
for the beef. This dish is delicious
accompanied with mashed potatoes
made with plenty of extra-virgin olive
oil instead of butter. 🌿

PANFRIED BEEF IN
SPICY TOMATO SAUCE

4 boneless beef steaks (about 6 ounces each), preferably center-cut top
    round or bottom round beef, sliced about ¼ inch thick or pounded
    to ¼ inch if cut thicker
4 tablespoons olive oil
½ cup chopped yellow onion
1 teaspoon minced garlic
3 anchovy fillets, minced
1 cup dry white wine
1½ cups peeled, seeded, drained, and chopped ripe or canned plum tomato
2 tablespoons minced fresh parsley, preferably flat-leaf type
2 teaspoons minced fresh oregano, or 1 teaspoon crumbled dried oregano
Salt
Freshly ground black pepper
Crushed dried hot chile
Fresh oregano sprigs or parsley sprigs, preferably flat-leaf type,
    for garnish (optional)

Quickly rinse the beef under running cold water and pat dry with paper toweling.
Set aside.

In a heavy-bottomed sauté pan or skillet, heat 2 tablespoons of the olive oil over
high heat. Add the beef and cook, turning once, until browned, 1½ to
2 minutes on each side. Remove the meat to a plate.

Add the remaining 2 tablespoons olive oil to the pan and place over medium heat.
Add the onion and sauté until soft but not browned, about 5 minutes. Add the
garlic and anchovies and cook for about 1 minute longer. Increase the heat to high,
add the wine and scrape up any browned bits from the pan bottom. Cook, stirring
frequently, until the wine is reduced by half, about 3 minutes. Stir in the tomato,
minced parsley, minced or dried oregano, and salt, pepper, and chile to taste. Cook,
stirring occasionally, until thickened, about 5 minutes. If desired, transfer to a food
processor fitted with a metal blade and coarsely purée, then return the sauce to the
pan.

Return the meat to the pan and cook, turning the meat in the sauce several times,
until the meat is heated through, 2 to 3 minutes. Transfer to a warmed serving
dish, garnish with oregano or parsley sprigs (if used), and serve immediately.

Makes 4 servings.

FEGATO ALLA VENEZIANA

LIVER AND ONIONS, VENETIAN STYLE

Due to health considerations, I limit my consumption of liver to rare occasions. This is my favorite preparation when I do indulge. I prefer the onion cooked longer and sweeter than what is recommended in most traditional versions of this memorable combination. Even friends who say they hate liver have been known to change their minds when they taste the velvety tender meat and the creamy onions.

Polenta is usually served alongside the liver. Although the Venetians reserve polenta made from white cornmeal for accompanying fish and poultry dishes, I chose to include it here to match the serving plate. ❧

LIVER AND ONIONS, VENETIAN STYLE

3 tablespoons vegetable oil
2 tablespoons unsalted butter
3 cups thinly sliced yellow onion
1 pound calf liver, sliced ¼ inch thick
Salt
Freshly ground black pepper
Minced fresh parsley, preferably flat-leaf type, for garnish

In a large, heavy-bottomed sauté pan or skillet, combine 2 tablespoons of the oil and 1 tablespoon of the butter over medium heat. When the butter stops foaming, add the onion and cook, stirring frequently, until the onion is soft and golden but not yet caramelized, about 40 minutes.

Meanwhile, cut the liver slices into pieces about 1 inch wide and 3 to 4 inches long. Remove and discard any white tubes that may run through the liver and trim away all traces of silvery membrane that would shrink during cooking and cause the liver to curl. Sprinkle with salt and pepper; set aside.

When the onion is ready, season with salt and pepper to taste. Using a slotted utensil, remove to a bowl and cover to keep warm.

Add the remaining 1 tablespoon each butter and oil to the same pan. Place over high heat. Just before the butter browns, add as many of the liver pieces as will fit comfortably without crowding. Cook just until the raw color disappears on the bottom, less than 1 minute. Using tongs, turn and cook the other side until lightly browned, only a few seconds longer. Remove the liver to the bowl containing the onion. Brown the remaining liver in the same manner. When all of the liver is cooked, return it and the onion to the pan still over high heat and toss briefly until heated through. Sprinkle with parsley and serve immediately.

Makes 4 servings.

BOLLITO MISTO
MIXED POACHED MEATS

A few Italian restaurants still roll out carts laden with huge cuts of various poached meats, including veal breast, tongue, and whole chicken, which are carved up at tableside. To turn this venerable tradition from Lombardy and Piedmont into something manageable at home, I start with individually sized pieces. Substitute any assortment of meats or poultry you like. The addition of vegetables and beans is a California update.

Although the Italian name means "mixed boil," the meats would get tough if allowed actually to boil, so keep them barely simmering. As a bonus, you'll have lots of flavorful broth left over for making soup, polenta, or risotto. 🌶

Tuscan White Beans (page 101)
2 quarts (8 cups) Italian-Style Broth (page 157), made from both meat and chicken, or 4 cups canned beef broth, preferably reduced-sodium type, diluted with 4 cups water
1 large yellow onion
1 large fennel bulb or 2 celery stalks
2 or 3 carrots, peeled
3 fresh parsley sprigs
2 bay leaves
12 pieces oxtail (about 2 pounds)
1½ pounds beef top round, trimmed of all excess fat and connective tissue and cut into 6 equal pieces
6 chicken thighs
2 cups peeled, seeded, drained, and chopped fresh or canned plum tomato
6 hot or mild Italian sausages
24 pearl onions
18 whole baby carrots, peeled
18 whole small turnips, peeled
12 fresh sage leaves, or 1 tablespoon crumbled dried sage
Salt
Freshly ground black pepper

The day before serving, prepare the white beans. Cover and refrigerate 3 cups of the beans; reserve the remaining beans for another purpose.

In a large stockpot, combine the broth, onion, fennel or celery, 2 or 3 carrots, parsley, and bay leaves. Place over high heat and bring to a boil. Add the oxtail and beef pieces, reduce the heat to a simmer, cover, and cook for about 2 hours, skimming and discarding all scum that rises to the surface. Add the chicken thighs and tomato and continue to simmer, covered, until the meats are very tender, about 1 hour longer. Remove the meats to a platter and strain the broth into a clean pan, pressing against the solids to release all the flavorful liquid.

Meanwhile, in a skillet, combine the sausages and water to cover and place over medium heat. Poach until done; slit with a small knife to check for doneness. Drain and reserve.

To peel the pearl onions, cut a small X in the root end of each onion. Bring a large pot three-fourths full of water to a boil over high heat. Drop the onions into the water. After about 30 seconds, drain the onions. As soon as they are cool enough to handle, pull off the skin and detach the roots; be careful not to remove any of the onion layers.

Place the pan with the broth over medium-high heat. Add the pearl onions, baby carrots, turnips, and sage and bring to a boil. Cover and cook until the vegetables are tender, about 20 minutes. Add the reserved meats, sausages, and white beans. Season to taste with salt and pepper. Simmer until all ingredients are heated through, about 5 minutes.

To serve, using a slotted utensil, distribute the meats and vegetables evenly among individual shallow bowls. Ladle a little broth over the meats and vegetables and serve immediately.

Makes 6 servings.

Tuscan White Beans

1 pound dried white beans, preferably imported *cannellini*
1 cup fresh sage leaves, tough stems discarded
1 teaspoon minced or pressed garlic
2 tablespoons extra-virgin olive oil
Salt
Freshly ground black pepper
Extra-virgin olive oil for serving

Carefully pick over the beans to remove any bits of foreign matter or shriveled beans. Place in a large bowl and add cold water to cover by about 3 inches. Let stand for 12 hours.

Drain the beans and transfer them to a heavy-bottomed saucepan. Add the sage, garlic (if used), olive oil, and enough water to cover by about ½ inch; stir well. Place over medium-low heat and bring to a boil. Reduce the heat to low, cover, and simmer, stirring occasionally, until the beans are very tender but still hold their shape and have absorbed most of the water, about 1 hour. Alternatively, combine the drained beans, sage, garlic (if used), oil, and water in an ovenproof dish, preferably made of earthenware. Cover tightly, transfer to an oven preheated to 225°F, and cook until done, about 2 hours.

Drain off excess water; the beans should be moist but not soupy. Season to taste with salt and pepper and serve. Diners should drizzle their servings with a little olive oil.

Makes 6 to 8 servings.

White Beans and Tomato Variation (*Fagioli all'uccelletto*). Cook and drain the beans as directed. In a skillet, heat ½ cup olive oil, preferably extra-virgin. Add 4 ounces Italian bacon (*pancetta*), chopped, and sauté until the bacon is lightly browned, about 4 minutes. Add 2 teaspoons minced garlic and cook for about 1 minute longer. Stir in 2 cups peeled, seeded, drained, and chopped ripe or canned tomato and cook for about 3 minutes. Add the beans and season to taste with salt and pepper. Place over medium-low heat and cook, stirring occasionally, until the liquid has thickened, about 20 minutes. If the mixture becomes too dry, stir in a little water or broth.

Fagioli alla Toscana
Tuscan White Beans

These Tuscan beans have many uses: They can be served as an antipasto on their own or combined with canned tuna, as a side dish, or contorno, or as an addition to soups and stews. The variation with tomatoes, which translates as "beans cooked like birds," is my favorite way to serve them. ❧

101

SWEET-AND-SOUR ONIONS

CIPOLLE IN AGRODOLCE

SWEET-AND-SOUR ONIONS

Serve these little golden beauties alongside poultry or meats, or add them to a plate of mixed antipasti. ❧

3 pounds pearl onions
3 tablespoons unsalted butter
1 cup golden raisins
¼ cup white wine vinegar
2 teaspoons sugar
Salt
Freshly ground black pepper

To peel the onions, cut a small *X* in the root end of each onion. Bring a large pot three-fourths full of water to a boil over high heat. Drop the onions into the water. After about 30 seconds, drain the onions. As soon as they are cool enough to handle, pull off the skin and detach the roots; be careful not to remove any of the onion layers.

In a heavy-bottomed sauté pan or skillet in which the onions will fit in a single layer, melt the butter over medium heat. Add the onions and sauté until they are well coated with the butter. Add water to a depth of 1 inch. Cook, turning the onions occasionally, until they begin to soften, about 10 minutes.

Add the raisins, vinegar, sugar, and salt and pepper to taste and stir well. Reduce the heat to low and simmer, stirring occasionally, until the onions are tender when pierced with a wooden skewer, 45 minutes to 1 hour, depending upon the size of the onions. If the pan becomes dry during cooking, add a tablespoon or so of water as needed. Increase the heat to medium-high and cook the onions, turning once or twice, until most of the liquid evaporates and the onions are glazed and golden, about 5 minutes. Adjust the seasonings. Transfer to a warmed serving dish and serve hot.

Makes 6 servings.

SPINACI E RABARBARO IN PADELLA

SAUTÉED SPINACH AND RHUBARB

I've never enjoyed spinach as much as when it was accented with tart rhubarb at Ristorante Peck in Milan. Here's my re-creation of that unique treatment of one of Italy's most popular vegetables.

For a classic Italian spinach preparation, omit the rhubarb. ❧

104

3 pounds young, tender spinach
2 tablespoons extra-virgin olive oil
2 tablespoons unsalted butter
2 garlic cloves, slightly crushed
4 ounces rhubarb, cut into matchsticks
1 teaspoon freshly squeezed lemon juice, or to taste
Salt
Freshly ground black pepper
Fresh lemon zest for garnish

Wash the spinach carefully to remove any sand or grit and discard any tough stems. Transfer the damp spinach to a saucepan. Cover the pan and place over medium heat. Cook, stirring occasionally, until the spinach is wilted, about 5 minutes. Drain in a colander and squeeze out as much liquid as possible. Set aside.

In a heavy-bottomed sauté pan or skillet, combine the olive oil, butter, and garlic. Place over medium heat and cook, stirring, until the garlic is browned, 2 to 3 minutes. Using a slotted utensil, remove and discard the garlic. Add the rhubarb and spinach and sauté until the rhubarb is crisp-tender and the spinach is heated through, 2 to 3 minutes. Season with lemon juice, salt, and pepper to taste. Garnish with lemon zest and serve immediately.

Makes 4 servings.

NOTE: To make the curly lemon zest garnish as shown, cut the peel from a lemon with a citrus zester in a long continuous strip. Wind the zest around a drinking straw, wrap in plastic wrap, and refrigerate for about 30 minutes. Just before serving, unwrap and slide out the straw.

SFORMATI DI VERDURA
VEGETABLE CUSTARDS

These soufflélike custards can be made with whatever fresh vegetables are available from the garden or market. In the photograph, clockwise from the top right, are custards made from green pattypan squash, carrot, cauliflower, broccoli, red sweet peppers, and yellow crookneck squash.

Serve on special occasions as an appetizer or as an accompaniment. ❦

106

Softened butter for greasing molds
About 1 pound fresh vegetables, trimmed, steamed or boiled
   until tender, and drained well
1 cup milk
1 cup heavy (whipping) cream
4 eggs
¼ cup all-purpose flour

¼ cup freshly grated parmesan cheese (about 1 ounce),
   preferably Parmigiano-Reggiano
Salt
Freshly ground black or white pepper
Freshly grated nutmeg
Fresh herb sprigs such as basil, mint, sage or thyme for garnish (optional)
Pesticide-free non-toxic flowers such as chive, lavender, or nasturtium
   blossoms for garnish (optional)

Preheat an oven to 375°F. Butter eight 1-cup ovenproof molds or ramekins; set aside.

Working in batches if necessary, place the cooked vegetables in a food processor fitted with a metal blade or in a blender and process until smooth. You should have about 2 cups. Transfer the vegetable purée to a bowl. Add the milk, cream, eggs, flour, cheese, and salt, pepper, and nutmeg to taste. Stir to mix well.

Distribute the vegetable mixture evenly among the prepared molds, using about ¾ cup for each container.

Transfer the molds to an ovenproof pan, place the pan in the oven, and pour in enough hot (not boiling) water to reach about two thirds of the way up the sides of the molds. Bake until a knife inserted in the center of the custard comes out barely clean, about 30 minutes. Remove the molds to a wire rack to cool for about 15 minutes.

To serve, run a thin, flexible knife blade around the inside of each mold and invert directly onto an individual plate. Garnish with herbs and/or flowers (if used). Serve immediately or at room temperature.

Makes 8 servings.

POTATO AND GREEN BEAN SALAD

About 2 quarts water
Salt
8 ounces small green beans, trimmed
1 pound medium-sized boiling (waxy) potatoes
About 2 tablespoons red wine vinegar
Freshly ground black pepper
¼ cup slivered red onion
About ¼ cup extra-virgin olive oil
1 to 2 tablespoon(s) minced fresh basil or oregano, chives, or
   parsley, preferably flat-leaf type, or a combination
½ teaspoon minced garlic (optional)

In a large pot, combine the water and about 2 teaspoons salt and bring to a boil over high heat. Add the beans and cook until crisp-tender, about 5 minutes for young, tender beans or considerably longer for older, tougher beans. Drain and rinse under running cold water to halt cooking. Set aside in a bowl.

Wash the potatoes under running cold water, scrubbing well to remove all traces of soil. Place in a saucepan and add water to cover by 2 inches, then remove the potatoes. Bring the water to a boil over medium-high heat, add the potatoes, and cook until just tender when pierced with a wooden skewer or small, sharp knife, 20 to 25 minutes; avoid overcooking. Drain, return the potatoes to the pan over medium heat, and shake the pan until excess moisture evaporates and the potatoes are dry to the touch. Remove the potatoes and set aside to cool slightly.

When the potatoes are cool enough to handle, peel them and cut crosswise into ⅜-inch-thick slices. Arrange the slices in a circle around the outside of a serving plate, slightly overlapping them. Sprinkle with vinegar, salt, and pepper to taste and let stand for about 5 minutes.

Add the onion to the beans and toss to mix. Sprinkle with salt and pepper to taste and 1 tablespoon of the vinegar, or to taste. Toss well, then add enough olive oil (about 2 tablespoons) to coat the beans lightly and toss again. Mound the beans in the center of the potato platter. Sprinkle the minced herb(s) and the garlic (if used) over the potatoes and beans. Drizzle the potatoes generously with olive oil and let stand for about 10 minutes before serving.

Makes 4 servings.

INSALATA DI PATATA E FAGIOLINO

POTATO AND GREEN BEAN SALAD

It is best to make this salad just before it is served, allowing only enough time for the vegetables to cool to room temperature and then stand for several minutes. If made too far in advance, the beans will turn dark and the potatoes will become mushy. Serve it alongside or following a second course of meat, poultry, or fish. It also makes a good antipasto. ❧

109

INSALATA D'ERBA FRESCA

FRESH HERB SALAD

In the mid-sixteenth century, Giacomo Castelvetro lived in England where he wrote of the garden-fresh produce of his native Italy in an attempt to convince the British to eat more vegetables and fruits. He lovingly described his favorite springtime salad: a melange of fresh herbs, tender greens, and blossoms. Like most other Italian cookery writers through the centuries, he called for plenty of salt (after all, the word insalata *means "in salt"), a generous amount of good olive oil, and a mere splash of vinegar.*

This same basic method can be used for preparing a salad that includes only one or more lettuces, as well as raw or lightly cooked vegetables. 🍅

About 5 cups mixed fresh young herb leaves or sprigs such as basil, borage, fennel, lemon balm, mint, salad burnet, tarragon, and watercress
About 3 cups mixed young greens such as arugula, chicory, lettuce, sorrel, and spinach
About 1 cup pesticide-free edible flowers such as borage, daylily petals, geraniums, miniature marigolds, nasturtiums, violas, and violets
Salt
Extra-virgin olive oil
Red wine vinegar or balsamic vinegar

Separate the herbs and lettuces into individual leaves. If the leaves are large, tear them into bite-sized pieces either before washing or just before serving. Remove the tough lower stems from the herbs. Wash the greens under running cold water. Or fill a basin with cold water, immerse the greens, and agitate the greens in the water to rinse well. Allow any grit or soil to settle to the bottom of the basin, then remove the greens. Drain off the water and repeat the process until the water is clear.

Transfer the wet greens to a salad spinner and spin to remove as much water as possible. Pat dry with paper toweling. Alternatively, wrap the greens in a cloth towel and shake vigorously to remove moisture, then pat dry with paper toweling. Wrap the dried greens in a clean cloth towel or in paper toweling and refrigerate for at least 30 minutes or for up to several hours to crisp.

For presentation, arrange the greens attractively in a salad bowl with plenty of room for tossing. At the table, sprinkle the "bouquet" with salt to taste, drizzle with oil, and toss thoroughly; use only enough oil to coat the greens lightly. Sprinkle with vinegar to taste, toss lightly but thoroughly, and serve immediately.

Makes 4 servings.

The fragrant anise flavor of fennel combines well with bitter greens and sweet oranges in this refreshing salad to follow a second course. ☙

FENNEL AND ORANGE SALAD

3 cups mixed tender bitter greens such as radicchio, Belgian endive, curly chicory, or frisée
3 oranges, preferably blood oranges
1 fennel bulb
Olive oil, preferably extra-virgin
Freshly squeezed lemon juice
Salt
Freshly ground black pepper

Wash the greens under running cold water. Place in a salad spinner and spin to remove as much water as possible. Pat dry with paper toweling. Alternatively, wrap the greens in a cloth towel and shake vigorously to remove moisture, then pat dry with paper toweling. Wrap the dried greens in a clean cloth towel or in paper toweling and refrigerate for at least 30 minutes or for up to several hours to crisp.

Peel the oranges, removing all the white pith. Slice crosswise. Set aside.

Trim the fennel bulb and then thinly slice. Set aside.

Transfer the crisp greens to a bowl. Drizzle lightly with olive oil and toss to coat. Add lemon juice, salt, and pepper to taste and toss lightly but thoroughly.

Arrange the greens on a serving platter or distribute among 4 individual plates. Arrange the fennel and orange slices over the greens. Drizzle the slices with a little olive oil and lemon juice. Serve immediately.

Makes 4 servings.

ENDINGS

CHEESES

(*Formaggi*)

—

FRUITS

(*Frutte*)

—

SWEETS

(*Dolci*)

—

AFTER-MEAL BEVERAGES

(*Caffè e Liquori*)

*F*ormal Italian meals call for at least one cheese to follow the salad course, so this section begins with a few suggestions for serving cheeses. Fortunately, wonderful imported Italian cheeses are now readily available from cheese shops, gourmet retailers, and even some supermarkets.

Most Italians prefer to end their meal with a piece or two of seasonal fruit. Pastries and other sweets are traditionally reserved for holidays and other special occasions, or for afternoon treats. I've included a few preparations made with fruit, followed by a small collection of my favorite Italian sweets that have not been included in my other cookbooks.

Although twice-baked cookies (*biscotti*), made for dunking in sweet wine or strong coffee, are often my choice for an ending to an Italian meal, I have chosen not to include a recipe, as there are now many excellent versions on the market. If these hard, long-lasting cookies are not found in specialty food stores or bakeries in your area, consult one of several good new books on the subject, or try the unusual version made with cornmeal in my *Corn Cookbook*.

Coffee, actually espresso, usually follows the fruit or sweet instead of accompanying it. Although Italians prefer coffee drinks made with milk in the morning or afternoon instead of after meals, I've included directions for preparing cappuccino and *caffèlatte* along with a discussion on espresso.

A wide range of Italian *liquori* may be offered with or following the espresso.

SERVING ITALIAN CHEESES

When the occasion calls for a special cheese presentation, consider one of these favorites.

For cheese in olive oil, thinly slice some creamy fresh mozzarella, aged or smoked provolone, or soft Fontina or Taleggio and arrange in shallow dishes. Pour extra-virgin olive oil over the top and add a few twists of black pepper from a mill. Cover and let stand overnight. Serve at room temperature.

For honeyed cheese, spoon sweet Gorgonzola onto cored pear halves, then drizzle with honey. Or offer a wedge of Gorgonzola accompanied by slices of walnut bread, fresh figs, and high-quality honey. Guests spread the cheese on the bread, top it with sliced or halved figs, and drizzle honey over the top.

For coffee-flavored cheese, stir together high-quality freshly made ricotta, sugar, and finely ground espresso-roast coffee beans to taste. Spoon into bowls, goblets, or coffee cups, or mound in the center of dessert plates. Garnish with whole espresso beans or chocolate-dipped coffee beans and mint sprigs or scented geranium leaves.

There is no better ending to an Italian meal than a chunk of nutty Parmigiano-Reggiano for nibbling, or a wedge of creamy sweet Gorgonzola. A slice or wedge of only one cheese can be presented on individual plates, or an assortment of cheeses can be offered on a platter or board. Crusty bread usually accompanies the cheese. Serve cheese and bread alone if you plan on a sweet dessert or fruit preparation to follow. If the cheese course will be the finale to the meal, add fresh apples, grapes, pears, peaches, or other fruit. Or scatter shelled nuts along side the cheese.

Cheese should be enjoyed at room temperature, so be sure to remove it from the refrigerator about an hour ahead of serving time, leaving it covered to prevent the surface from drying out. ❧

MACEDONIA DI FRUTTA

MACERATED FRESH FRUIT COMPOTE

*D*on't skip over this recipe because it seems too simple. A hallmark of the Italian kitchen, it remains one of Italy's most popular and refreshing desserts.

Choose only fruit that is in season and perfectly ripe. Among the possibilities are peeled and pitted or seeded apricots, mangoes, nectarines, papayas, peaches, or soft pears; fresh berries; seedless grapes; peeled kiwifruits; pitted cherries; orange and tangerine segments; and melons. I prefer to use apples and crisp pears in other ways and find their crunchiness unappealing in a fruit compote.

If adding berries, kiwifruits, or bananas to the compote, do so at the last minute to prevent them from becoming soggy; also, berries will stain the other fruits with color and bananas will turn brown. 🍎

MACERATED FRESH FRUIT COMPOTE

2 cups freshly squeezed orange juice
Grated or minced zest of 1 lemon or lime
Juice of 1 lemon or lime
2 pounds assorted fresh fruit (see recipe introduction),
  cut into bite-sized pieces
½ cup sugar, or to taste
Italian anise-, cherry-, or orange-flavored liqueur (optional)

In a large bowl, combine the orange juice and lemon or lime zest and juice. Add the fruit. (If using berries, kiwifruits, or bananas, toss those in just before serving.) Toss to coat well with the citrus juices to prevent discoloration. Add sugar and liqueur (if used) to taste. Cover tightly and refrigerate for at least several hours or as long as overnight; stir several times to blend well.

To serve, spoon the fruits and juices into individual dishes.

Makes 6 servings.

VENETIAN GLAZED ORANGES

*T*his simple recipe turns fresh

oranges into something extra

special. ☙

120

8 navel oranges or blood oranges
2 cups sugar
1 cup water
1 cup freshly squeezed orange juice
¼ cup freshly squeezed lemon juice
About ¼ cup Italian maraschino liqueur or kirsch (optional)
Fresh mint sprigs for garnish (optional)

Using a vegetable peeler, remove enough of the zest (the colored part of the peel with none of the bitter white pith) from the oranges in long, thin julienne strips to measure ½ cup.

Cut away the peel and all of the white membrane from the oranges, keeping them as round as possible. Set aside.

In a saucepan or other nonreactive pot large enough to hold all of the oranges, combine the sugar, water, orange and lemon juices, and the orange zest. Place over medium-high heat and bring to a gentle boil. Cook until the mixture is thickened to a thin syrup consistency, 5 to 8 minutes.

Add the oranges to the syrup and continue cooking, turning the oranges frequently to coat evenly with the syrup, for 5 minutes. Remove from the heat and stir in the liqueur (if used). Set aside to cool.

Cover and chill the oranges for at least 2 hours or as long as overnight, turning them occasionally in the syrup.

Return almost to room temperature before serving. Spoon into a serving dish or individual dishes and garnish with mint sprigs (if used).

Makes 8 servings.

BAKED STUFFED PEACHES

Softened butter for greasing baking dish
6 large, ripe but firm freestone peaches
½ cup Italian almond macaroons (*amaretti*), finely crushed
   (about 20 small imported cookies)
⅓ cup almonds, toasted and finely chopped
¼ cup unsweetened cocoa powder (optional)
¼ cup sugar, if using cocoa powder
1 tablespoon freshly grated or minced lemon zest
Italian almond liqueur (Amaretto), as needed
About 1 tablespoon unsalted butter, cut into bits
1 to 2 tablespoons sugar for sprinkling
12 small fresh mint leaves for garnish
Mascarpone cheese (optional)

In a large saucepan, add enough water to cover the peaches amply when added later. Place over high heat and bring to a gentle boil.

Meanwhile, preheat an oven to 400°F. Butter a shallow baking dish; set aside.

Drop the peaches into the boiling water for about 1 minute. Transfer to a colander to drain. As soon as the peaches are cool enough to handle, pull off the skins, then split in half vertically and remove stones. Using a small, sharp knife and a spoon, carve out the peaches, removing enough of the pulp to leave a shell about ½ inch thick.

In a bowl, combine the scooped-out peach pulp with the crushed macaroons, chopped almonds, cocoa (if used), the ¼ cup sugar (if using cocoa), and lemon zest. Add enough of the liqueur to form a thick paste.

Divide the stuffing mixture evenly among the peach halves. Place the peaches in the prepared baking dish, dot with the butter, and lightly sprinkle with sugar. Bake until the peaches are tender but still hold their shape, about 15 minutes.

Garnish each peach half with a mint leaf. Serve warm or at room temperature with dollops of mascarpone, if desired.

Makes 6 servings.

*PESCHE RIPIENE AL
FORNO*

BAKED STUFFED PEACHES

I've served these peaches frequently during peach season ever since I tried them on my first Italian sojourn some two decades ago. ❧

FRESH FIG TART

CROSTATA DI FICHI
FRESH FIG TART

*L*ike so many things that look and
taste French to us, the origins of tarts
such as this are definitely Italian.
Substitute other seasonal fruit or
berries, one kind or in combination,
to create a variety of tarts. The
mascarpone, *a thick Italian cream
cheese, adds an extra touch of
richness; there is no substitute.* ❧

TART PASTRY (*PASTA FROLLA*)
1¼ cups all-purpose flour
¼ cup sugar
⅛ teaspoon salt
1 teaspoon grated or minced fresh lemon zest
½ cup (1 stick) unsalted butter, frozen or very cold, cut into small pieces
1 egg yolk
2 to 3 tablespoons iced water, or as necessary

PASTRY CREAM (*CREMA PASTICCERIA*)
3 egg yolks
¼ cup sugar
¼ cup all-purpose flour
1⅓ cups milk
1 teaspoon pure vanilla extract

About 20 fresh figs
1 cup *mascarpone*
½ cup fig or apricot preserves or orange or lemon marmalade, chopped
½ teaspoon orange-flavored liqueur

To make the pastry, place the flour, sugar, salt, lemon zest, and butter in a food processor fitted with a metal blade. Pulse until well blended and the consistency of cornmeal. With the machine running, add the egg yolk through the feed tube and just enough of the iced water, about 1 teaspoon at a time, until the dough begins to gather into a rough mass. Alternatively, combine the flour, sugar, salt, lemon zest, and butter in a bowl and, using a pastry blender or your fingertips, work the ingredients together until the mixture resembles cornmeal. Then, using a fork, blend in the egg yolk and enough of the iced water to form a rough mass.

Working quickly, form the dough into a ball, place in the center of a 9-inch tart pan or springform pan and press into a flat disk. Using your fingertips, press the dough onto the bottom and sides of the pan or dish to cover evenly, about 1/8 inch thick. Smooth the top rim or crimp the edges to form an attractive pattern. Cover tightly and refrigerate or freeze until thoroughly chilled, about 2 hours.

To make the pastry cream, in a saucepan, using a wire whisk or electric mixer, beat together the egg yolks and sugar until thoroughly incorporated. Add the flour and beat until smooth.

Meanwhile, in a saucepan, heat the milk almost to the boiling point. Add the milk, a little at a time, to the egg mixture, whisking constantly. Place over low heat and cook, stirring constantly, until the custard thickens enough to coat the back of a spoon, then continue cooking and stirring until quite thick, about 3 minutes longer.

Recipe continues on page 126.

Remove from the heat and set aside to cool slightly, then stir in the vanilla. Cover with a piece of plastic wrap or waxed paper, pressing it directly onto the surface of the custard to prevent a skin from forming. Refrigerate until well chilled, about 1 hour or for up to 24 hours.

Preheat an oven to 375°F.

Line the chilled crust with foil, allowing the foil to hang over the edges of the crust to prevent browning too fast. Fill the foil-lined crust with ceramic or metal pie weights, dried beans, or rice. Bake for 15 minutes, then remove the weights and foil and continue baking until the crust is golden brown, 10 to 15 minutes longer. Transfer to a wire rack to cool completely, then remove the tart shell from the pan to a serving plate.

Shortly before assembling the tart, cut the figs in half, into quarters, or into slices and place in a bowl.

In a bowl, combine the chilled pastry cream and the mascarpone. Using an electric mixer or a wire whisk, beat until the mixture is smooth. Spread the mixture in an even layer in the cooled pastry shell. Arrange the figs in an attractive pattern over the custard layer.

In a small saucepan, heat the preserves over medium heat until melted, then stir in the liqueur. Brush lightly over the figs. Serve at room temperature within an hour.

Makes 8 servings.

SIENESE SPICE CAKE

1 cup Candied Orange Zest (page 161) or a high-quality commercial
   product (available in specialty food stores)
Unsalted butter for greasing parchment paper
1 cup hazelnuts (about 4 ounces)
1 cup blanched almonds (about 6 ounces)
1 cup chopped high-quality glazed apricots, citron, or other fruit
   (about 8 ounces)
4 teaspoons freshly minced or grated lemon zest
1 teaspoon ground cinnamon
½ teaspoon freshly grated nutmeg
½ teaspoon ground aniseed
½ teaspoon ground coriander
¼ teaspoon ground cloves
¼ teaspoon freshly ground white pepper
1 cup all-purpose flour
½ cup honey
¾ cup granulated sugar
2 tablespoons unsalted butter, melted
Powdered sugar for dusting

Prepare the Candied Orange Zest at least several hours or up to a few days before
making the cake. If using purchased candied zest, set aside.

Preheat an oven to 325°F. Cut a square of baking parchment large enough to line
the bottom and sides of a 9-inch springform pan. Line the pan, cutting off the
excess paper even with the top of the pan. Generously grease the parchment with
butter.

Pour the hazelnuts and almonds into separate shallow ovenproof pans. Place in the
upper portion of the oven and toast, stirring occasionally, until the nuts are
fragrant, 10 to 15 minutes. Pour the hazelnuts onto a heavy clean cloth towel, fold
the towel over the nuts, and rub the nuts vigorously to remove as much of the skins
as possible; don't worry about areas that will not come off easily. Pour the almonds
onto a plate to cool.

Coarsely chop the hazelnuts and almonds and transfer to a large bowl. Chop the
reserved candied zest and add to the nuts. Add the glazed fruit, lemon zest,
cinnamon, nutmeg, aniseed, coriander, cloves, and white pepper. Add the flour
and mix thoroughly; set aside.

Combine the honey and granulated sugar and place over medium heat. Cook,
stirring frequently, until the mixture reaches about 245°F on a candy thermometer,
or until it forms a soft ball when a little bit of it is dropped into a bowl of cold
water. Pour the syrup over the nut-and-fruit mixture, add the melted butter, and

Recipe continues on page 128.

PANFORTE
SIENESE SPICE CAKE

Countless shop windows along the
narrow winding streets of Siena
display this local cake. The
Crusaders dubbed the dense cake
panforte, or "strong bread," because
it could be taken on long journeys
without spoiling. Thickly laced with
nuts and glazed fruit, the confection
was nearly heavy enough to double as
a weapon.

Instead of using the bland-tasting
candied fruit found in most
supermarkets, look for high-quality
imports from Italy, available in
specialty shops, especially in the fall;
honey-glazed apricots from Australia
are also wonderful. When stored in
an airtight container, panforte,
which is almost like a candy, will last
for up to a month.

127

stir the sticky dough until all the ingredients are thoroughly incorporated. Turn the mixture out into the prepared pan. Moisten fingers lightly with water and press out the dough to the edges of the pan to form an even layer.

Bake until the top of the cake is golden brown, 35 to 40 minutes; the gooey cake will not appear done but will set as it cools. Remove to a wire rack to cool for about 15 minutes. Remove the pan ring, then pick the cake up by the parchment paper and remove the pan bottom. Place the cake back on the rack to cool completely, at least 1 hour. After the cake is cold, invert it onto a plate and peel off and discard the parchment paper. Dust the top of the cake with powdered sugar. Cut into small wedges for serving.

Makes 12 servings.

SIENESE SPICE CAKE VARIATIONS

Chocolate Panforte (*Panforte di cioccolato*). Add 3 tablespoons unsweetened cocoa powder along with the flour. Invert the cooled cake onto a wire rack. Melt 6 ounces high-quality semisweet or bittersweet chocolate with 2 tablespoons unsalted butter; whisk until smooth and spread over the top of the cake. When the glaze has set completely, lightly dust with sweetened powdered cocoa, if desired.

Peppered Panforte (*Panpepato*). Prepare the Chocolate Panforte variation, increasing the white pepper to 1¼ teaspoons. Dust the finished cake with a mixture of equal parts powdered sugar and ground cinnamon or glaze with chocolate.

CHOCOLATE-GLAZED ALMOND FLORENTINES

Unsalted butter for greasing baking sheet
All-purpose flour for dusting baking sheet
¾ cup sliced almonds (about 4½ ounces)
¼ cup heavy (whipping) cream
⅓ cup sugar
¼ cup (½ stick) unsalted butter
¼ cup all-purpose flour
½ cup very finely chopped Candied Orange Zest (page 161)
6 ounces high-quality bittersweet or semisweet chocolate
1 teaspoon solid vegetable shortening

Preheat an oven to 350°F. Grease 1 or 2 baking sheet(s) with butter and dust with flour, shaking off excess. Set aside.

Place half of the almonds in a food processor fitted with a metal blade or in a blender and process until fine; do not process too long or the oil from the nuts will be released.

In a saucepan, combine the cream, sugar, and butter over low heat, stirring occasionally, until the butter melts. Increase the heat to medium-high and bring the mixture to a boil, then remove from the heat.

Stir the ground almonds and flour into the butter mixture to make a thin batter. Stir in the remaining sliced almonds and the orange zest.

Drop the batter by scant teaspoonfuls onto the prepared baking sheet(s) and flatten with the back of a spoon to about 1½ inches in diameter. Space the cookies about 2 inches apart.

Bake until the edges begin to brown, about 10 minutes. Remove the baking sheet(s) to a wire rack to cool until cookies become firm, 2 to 3 minutes. Using a spatula, transfer the cookies to a wire rack to cool completely.

When the cookies are cold, combine the chocolate and vegetable shortening in the top pan of a double boiler over hot (not boiling) water. Stir until the chocolate melts.

Turn the cookies over. Using a pastry brush, paint melted chocolate on the bottom of each cookie. Let dry for several hours until the chocolate hardens.

Store in a covered container in the refrigerator for up to 3 days or in the freezer for as long as 3 months.

Makes about 24 cookies.

BISCOTTI ALLA FIORENTINA

CHOCOLATE-GLAZED ALMOND FLORENTINES

Half candy and half cookie, these delicacies are rich and sweet and are excellent with good strong coffee. Food historians date them back to the fifteenth century.

CIAMBELLA

RUSTIC DUNKING CAKE

When *sharing her recipe, my friend Marian May wrote that "Of all the just-right tastes of Italian food, ciambella is one of my favorites. Whenever I make one of these rustic, hard, heavy, lumpy cakes, I think of the day before my daughter Nancy's wedding. We needed a snack after all that high-powered wedding-menu planning at Villa d'Este, so we stopped at a plane tree–canopied outdoor cafe in Cernobbio. As the October leaves billowed up around our ankles, we consumed hefty chunks of this wonderful ring cake dunked in glasses of rather sweet white wine."* ❦

132

Variations on this country cake are common throughout Italy. The cake is dipped into caffèlatte for a morning treat, and later in the day the slices are dunked in sweet wine. For the morning version, you might wish to substitute lemon juice for the wine and use lemon zest instead of aniseed.

Unsalted butter for greasing baking sheet
All-purpose flour for dusting baking sheet and work surface
2 cups all-purpose flour, or 4 cups all-purpose flour if corn flour is not used
2 cups corn flour or very finely ground cornmeal (optional)
⅔ cup sugar
2½ teaspoons cream of tartar
1 teaspoon baking soda
1 tablespoon aniseed, or to taste
5 tablespoons unsalted butter, melted
3 tablespoons olive oil
¼ cup milk
¼ cup sweet white wine
2 eggs

Preheat an oven to 375°F. Grease a baking sheet with softened butter and dust with flour, shaking off the excess. Set aside.

In a large bowl, combine the 2 or 4 cups flour, corn flour (if used), sugar, cream of tartar, baking soda, and aniseed. Add the melted butter, olive oil, milk, and wine. Stir to mix well.

In a small bowl, beat the eggs lightly, then set aside 1 teaspoon for glazing. Add the remaining egg to the flour mixture and stir ingredients together thoroughly. Turn the mixture out onto a lightly floured work surface and knead until the dough holds together in a compact mound, about 5 minutes. Plunge both thumbs into the center of the mound and pull the dough into a thick ring about 8 inches in diameter.

Center the dough ring on the prepared baking sheet and brush the top and sides with the reserved beaten egg. Bake until golden brown and a wooden skewer inserted into the cake comes out clean, about 30 minutes.

Transfer to a wire rack to cool completely. (The flavor of the cake improves on the second or third day after baking. Tightly wrapped and refrigerated, it keeps for about a week.) Cut into slices to serve.

Makes 8 to 10 servings.

SICILIAN FEAST CAKE

CASSATA ALLA SICILIANA

SICILIAN FEAST CAKE

I find this variation on the popular Sicilian specialty to be less cloying than the traditional one, which calls for a candied fruit–studded filling. A two-layer, 9-inch sponge cake may be used in place of the denser pound cake to create a lighter version. Use a favorite recipe for making either pound cake or sponge cake or purchase a high-quality cake. ❦

134

A pound cake, baked in a 5-by-9-inch loaf pan
1 pound high-quality ricotta cheese, preferably freshly made
  (available in Italian markets and some cheese shops)
½ cup powdered sugar
1 teaspoon instant espresso powder
2 tablespoons orange- or coffee-flavored liqueur or freshly squeezed orange juice
2 ounces high-quality bittersweet or semisweet chocolate, chopped into small pieces
1¼ cups chopped pistachios or blanched almonds (about 6 ounces)

CHOCOLATE-ESPRESSO ICING
8 ounces high-quality bittersweet or semisweet chocolate, chopped into small pieces
1 tablespoon instant espresso powder
1 cup heavy (whipping) cream
2 teaspoons pure vanilla extract
¾ cup powdered sugar, or to taste

Slice away and discard the crusts from the pound cake. Using a serrated knife, cut the cake horizontally into 3 equal layers. Transfer 1 layer to a serving plate.

In a food processor fitted with a metal blade, combine the ricotta, sugar, espresso powder, and liqueur or orange juice and beat until smooth. (Alternatively, pass the ricotta through a food mill into a bowl.) Fold in the chocolate pieces and ½ cup of the chopped nuts.

Spread one half of the ricotta mixture over the cake layer, then top with another layer of the cake, aligning the sides and ends. Spread with the remaining filling and top with the third cake layer. Press gently to make the cake compact, smoothing the filling and sides with a spatula. Cover with plastic wrap and refrigerate until the filling is firm, at least several hours or as long as overnight.

When the cake is thoroughly chilled, make the icing. Place a large metal mixing bowl in a larger bowl filled with ice and water. In a small pan, combine the chocolate, espresso powder, and cream and place over low heat until the chocolate melts. Whisk or stir until smooth. Stir in the vanilla. Transfer to the prepared mixing bowl. Using a wire whisk or an electric mixer, whisk or beat until the mixture forms a spreading consistency. While continuing to beat, gradually add powdered sugar to taste.

Using a spatula, spread the sides and top of the cake with the icing. Press the remaining ¾ cup pistachios or almonds into the sides of the cake. Chill until the icing is set, about 30 minutes. Cut into slices to serve.

Makes about 10 servings.

DOME CAKE

A pound cake baked in a 5-by-9-inch loaf pan
About ½ cup Frangelico (hazelnut liqueur)
1 cup hazelnuts (about 4 ounces)
2 cups heavy (whipping) cream
¼ cup powdered sugar
8 ounces high-quality semisweet chocolate, chopped

Place a metal bowl and a wire whisk or the beaters of a hand-held mixer in the freezer until well chilled.

Select a 1½-quart bowl with the roundest possible bottom. Line the bowl with a layer of dampened cheesecloth. Set aside.

Preheat an oven to 375°F.

Cut the cake vertically into slices about ⅜ inch thick, then cut each slice on the diagonal into 2 pieces to form triangles. Spiraling out from the center of the bottom of the cheesecloth-lined bowl, line the bowl with the cake pieces. Reserve the remaining cake pieces. Brush the cake in the bowl with the liqueur. Set aside.

Pour the hazelnuts into a shallow ovenproof pan. Place in the upper portion of the oven and toast, stirring occasionally, until the nuts are fragrant, 10 to 15 minutes. Pour onto a heavy clean cloth towel, fold the towel over the nuts, and rub the nuts vigorously to remove as much of the skins as possible; don't worry about areas that will not come off easily. Chop the nuts and set aside.

Remove the chilled bowl from the freezer and pour the cream into it. Add the sugar and, using the chilled whisk or beaters, beat until fairly stiff. Fold the chopped hazelnuts and 2 ounces of the chocolate into the cream. Using half of the mixture, spoon the whipped cream over the cake in the bowl, leaving an indention in the center.

Place the remaining 6 ounces chocolate in a small, heat-resistant glass bowl set over (not touching) simmering water and stir frequently until melted. Alternatively, place the chocolate in a microwave-safe bowl and place in a microwave oven, stopping and stirring every 30 seconds, until melted. Cool the chocolate, then stir it into the remaining whipped cream mixture and spoon the mixture into the center of the cake

Working with one at a time, brush each remaining cake triangle with the liqueur and place it atop the cake filling to cover completely. Cut away any exposed cake lining the bowl evenly with the new top cake layer. Cut small pieces of cake to fill any holes in the top layer. Cover with plastic wrap and refrigerate at least overnight or for up to 2 days.

To serve, invert the cake onto a serving plate. Peel off the cheesecloth. Cut into wedges at the table.

Makes 8 servings.

ZUCCOTTO
DOME CAKE

During a recent visit to Florence, I had to search for the few places that still offer this classic dessert of the Renaissance city. Food historians cannot agree as to whether the heavenly confection is named for the dome of the city's cathedral, for the dome-shaped hats worn by cardinals, or for the less holy but equally lofty pumpkin.

Most recipes call for maraschino liqueur or a mixture of spirits, as well as at least two kinds of nuts. I prefer the simplicity and consistency of hazelnut liqueur and chopped hazelnuts, especially with the intense chocolate of the inner layer. Use a favorite recipe for making the pound cake, or purchase a high-quality cake. Or for a more delicate result, use a two-layer, 9-inch round sponge cake. ❦

137

COOKED CREAM

PANNA COTTA
COOKED CREAM

*T*he very few written recipes that
I've seen for this favorite dessert of
Tuscany and Piedmont call for
heating half of the cream, then
cooling it before whipping the
remaining cream and folding the two
together with softened gelatin. To my
taste, this creates a texture more akin
to a Bavarian cream than to the silky
quivering versions of panna cotta
I've enjoyed in Italy. This one is
reminiscent of the version served at
Osteria del Cinghiale Bianco in
Florence. ❦

1 envelope (1 scant tablespoon) unflavored gelatin
¼ cup milk
3 cups heavy (whipping) cream
½ cup sugar
Softened unsalted butter for greasing molds

FRESH BERRY SAUCE
2 cups blackberries, raspberries, or strawberries, or a combination
1 teaspoon balsamic vinegar or freshly squeezed lemon juice, or to taste
3 tablespoons sugar, or to taste

**Fresh strawberries, preferably small wild variety, or a mixture of fresh
  berries, for garnish**

In a small bowl, combine the gelatin and milk. Stir well and set aside to soften.

Meanwhile, in a saucepan over medium heat, combine the cream and sugar. Heat,
stirring frequently, until the mixture comes to a boil. Stir in the softened gelatin and
continue to stir until the mixture is smooth and the gelatin is completely dissolved,
about 1 minute. Pour into a large glass measuring cup or bowl. Cover with a piece
of plastic wrap or waxed paper, pressing it directly onto the surface of the cream to
prevent a skin from forming. Let cool to room temperature.

Lightly butter six 6-ounce custard cups or timbale molds. Pour or spoon the cooled
cream mixture into the prepared containers, distributing evenly. Cover tightly with
plastic wrap and refrigerate until set, at least 3 hours or as long as 12 hours.

To make the berry sauce, combine the berries and vinegar or lemon juice in a food
processor fitted with a metal blade or in a blender and process until very smooth.
Sweeten to taste with the sugar.

To serve, dip the base of each mold into hot water for about 30 seconds, run a knife
with a flexible blade around the inside of each mold, and invert directly onto an
individual plate. Spoon the sauce over the top and garnish with the berries.

Makes 6 servings.

Variations on page 140.

ITALIAN ICES VARIATIONS

Fruit Ice (*Granita di frutta*). Purée enough stemmed, fresh berries or peeled, pitted, and sliced ripe mangoes, melon, nectarines, peaches, pears, or persimmons to equal 2 cups purée (about 4 cups berries or sliced fruit). Combine the purée with about 2 tablespoons freshly squeezed lemon, lime, or orange juice and 1½ cups of the Simple Syrup, or to taste. Freeze as directed. Garnish servings with a few of the same berries or fruit slices used in the *granita*.

Coffee Ice (*Granita di caffè*). Combine 2½ cups cold, brewed espresso or other cold, freshly brewed dark-roast coffee and ½ cup of the Simple Syrup, or to taste. For *caffèlatte* ice, add heavy (whipping) cream to taste. Freeze as directed. Garnish servings with dollops of whipped cream, if desired.

Citrus Ice (*Granita di citrone*). Combine 1¾ cups freshly squeezed orange or tangerine juice, or a combination, 2 tablespoons freshly squeezed lemon juice, 2 teaspoons minced or grated fresh zest of the same fruit as the juice, and 1 cup of the Simple Syrup, or to taste. Freeze as directed. Garnish servings with fresh mint sprigs.

Grapefruit-Campari Ice (*Granita di pompelmo e campari*). Combine 2 cups freshly squeezed grapefruit juice, 1 teaspoon minced or grated fresh grapefruit zest, ¾ cup Campari, and 1 cup of the Simple Syrup, or to taste. Freeze as directed.

Lemon Ice (*Granita di limone*). Combine 1 cup cold water, ¾ cup freshly squeezed lemon juice, 2 teaspoons minced or grated fresh lemon zest, and 1¼ cups of the Simple Syrup, or to taste. Freeze as directed. Garnish servings with lemon slices and lemon leaves (if available).

GELATO DI CREMA
CUSTARD ICE CREAM

_M_y fondest gastronomic memories of visits to Italy are centered around this creamy concoction. On a hot September afternoon in the late 1970s, while waiting to meet up with dear friends from California who had been traveling separately from us, Lin and I sampled several flavors from Gelateria Vivoli, a Florence institution near Santa Croce. After Marian and Louis arrived, we all indulged in several other scoops of gelato, _including one containing grains of rice. It took a lot of sight-seeing to walk off our frozen feast._

On a recent trip I was pleased to discover that Vivoli's gelato still tastes as great as I remember. During our daily pilgrimages to the venerable institution, Andrew and I sampled many flavors, although crema, _the plain custard version, remains my favorite._ 🍎

Here is a basic custard recipe and a few flavor variations to get you started. If you have a large ice cream maker, you can double the recipe. Many Italian cookbooks do not call for cream in their gelato recipes, but it adds the smoothness and richness of products made in Italy.

2 cups milk
2 cups heavy (whipping) cream
Zest of 1 lemon
7 egg yolks
1 cup sugar
¼ teaspoon salt

In a saucepan, combine the milk, cream, and lemon zest. Place over medium heat and bring the mixture just to a simmer. Remove from the heat.

In a bowl, combine the egg yolks, sugar, and salt and, using a whisk or an electric mixer, beat until the mixture is pale yellow, about 3 minutes. Slowly stir the warm milk mixture into the beaten egg mixture. Transfer to the top pan of a double boiler placed over barely simmering water. Cook, stirring constantly with a wooden spoon, until the custard mixture reaches 180°F on a candy thermometer, or until it thickens enough to coat the back of the spoon thickly. This will take 15 to 20 minutes; do not allow to boil. Strain through a fine-mesh sieve into a bowl set in a pan of ice. Cover with a piece of plastic wrap or waxed paper, pressing it directly onto the top of the custard to prevent a skin from forming and let cool for about 15 minutes. Cover tightly and refrigerate until well chilled, at least 3 hours or, preferably, overnight.

Pour the chilled custard mixture into an ice cream maker and freeze according to the manufacturer's instructions. Serve when the gelato holds together but is still soft. Or pack into a container with a tight-fitting lid and place in a freezer for several hours or for up to several days. Transfer the freezer container to the refrigerator about 30 minutes before you plan to serve the ice cream to allow it to reach the proper consistency. If the gelato gets icy from long storage in a freezer, whip it with a wire whisk just before serving.

Makes about 1 quart, enough for 4 servings.

Variations on page 146.

144

REDUCED FAT ICE CREAM

*F*or *a noncustard-based fruit gelato,*
purée enough stemmed berries or
figs, peeled and pitted nectarines or
peaches, or other soft fruit to equal 2
cups purée. Transfer to a bowl. Add
1½ cups milk, 1 teaspoon pure
vanilla extract or almond extract,
and 1 cup Simple Syrup (page 141),
or to taste. Pour into an ice cream
maker and freeze according to the
146   *manufacturer's instructions.*

Makes about 1 quart, enough for 4
servings. ❧

Vanilla Ice Cream (*Gelato di vaniglia*). Omit the lemon zest. Split 1 vanilla bean and add to the milk and cream before bringing it to a simmer. Remove the vanilla bean halves and scrape the seeds from the pods into the heated cream. Also add 1 tablespoon pure vanilla extract to the cooled custard before refrigerating.

Caramel Ice Cream (*Gelato di caramello*). In a heavy saucepan, stir together 1 cup sugar and ¼ cup water until well mixed. (For a less pronounced caramel flavor, use ½ cup sugar and 2 tablespoons water.) Cover and place over medium-high heat until the sugar melts and bubbles, about 4 minutes. Remove the cover and occasionally swirl the pan or stir the mixture until the syrup is a rich amber, 5 to 8 minutes. While cooking, brush the sides of the pan with a wet brush just above the bubbling sugar to keep crystals from forming. Remove from the heat until the mixture stops boiling. While whisking or stirring, slowly add 1 cup of the cold cream; don't worry if the caramel syrup begins to harden. Place over low heat, stirring constantly, until smooth.

Heat the milk with the remaining 1 cup cream as directed in the basic recipe. Combine the eggs with only ¼ cup sugar and complete the custard. (If the reduced amount of caramelized sugar was used as noted above, use a total of ¾ cup sugar when beating with the eggs.) Stir the warm custard into the caramel mixture and strain into a cold container. Let cool, then stir in 2 teaspoons pure vanilla extract before refrigerating.

Chocolate Ice Cream (*Gelato di cioccolata*). Reduce the sugar to ½ cup and omit the lemon zest. Melt 6 to 8 ounces high-quality semisweet or bittersweet chocolate and stir into the warm custard. Let cool, then stir in 1 teaspoon pure vanilla extract. Alternatively, use the recommended amount of sugar and sift ¼ cup unsweetened cocoa powder, or more to taste, into the milk mixture and beat until smooth before bringing the mixture to a simmer. Stir the vanilla into the cooled custard before refrigerating.

Chocolate-Hazelnut Ice Cream (*Gelato di gianduia*). Omit the lemon zest. Finely chop or grind 2 cups hazelnuts and add to the milk mixture before bringing the mixture to a simmer. Remove the hot mixture from the heat and let stand for 30 minutes, then strain through a sieve lined with dampened cheesecloth, pressing the nuts with a wooden spoon to release all of the liquid. Pour the milk mixture into a saucepan and reheat. Prepare the custard as directed, then melt 4 ounces high-quality semisweet chocolate and stir it into the warm custard. Let cool, then stir in 1 teaspoon pure vanilla extract before refrigerating.

Coffee Ice Cream (*Gelato di caffè*). Omit the lemon zest. Dissolve 3 tablespoons instant espresso powder, or to taste, in the warm milk mixture.

Lemon Ice Cream (*Gelato di limone*). Add the zest of 2 more lemons and ½ cup freshly squeezed lemon juice to the milk and cream before bringing it to a simmer.

Nut Ice Cream (*Gelato di noce*). Finely chop or grind 2 cups toasted almonds, hazelnuts, pecans, pine nuts, or walnuts or roasted peanuts and add to the milk mixture before bringing it to a simmer. Remove from the heat and let stand for 30 minutes, then strain through a sieve lined with dampened cheesecloth, pressing the nuts with a wooden spoon to release all of the liquid. Pour the milk mixture into a saucepan and reheat. (For a textured ice cream, do not strain.) Continue as directed, adding 1 teaspoon pure vanilla extract or almond or other nut extract to the cooled custard before refrigerating.

Peach Ice Cream (*Gelato di pesca*). Peel, pit, and purée enough peaches to equal 2 cups purée. Stir into the cooled custard before refrigerating.

Rhubarb Ice Cream (*Gelato di rabarabaro*). In a heavy-bottomed saucepan, combine 2 quarts chopped rhubarb, ⅔ cup sugar, and ½ cup water. Place over medium heat and cook, stirring occasionally, until the rhubarb is very tender. Transfer to a food processor fitted with a metal blade or to a blender and purée. Stir in 2 table-spoons freshly squeezed lemon juice and set aside while you prepare the custard as directed. Stir the purée into the warm custard, then cool to room temperature before refrigerating.

Strawberry or Raspberry Ice Cream (*Gelato di fragola o gelato di lampone*). Using 3 egg yolks, prepare a half recipe of the basic custard and set aside to cool. In a food processor, purée about 6 cups berries. Measure purée to equal 3 cups. Stir in 2 tablespoons freshly squeezed lemon juice and sweeten to taste with sugar (½ to ¾ cup); the purée should taste slightly too sweet in order to account for reduced sweetness that results from the freezing process. Stir the purée into the cooled custard before refrigerating.

White Chocolate Ice Cream (*Gelato di cioccolata bianca*). Omit the lemon zest. Chop 1 pound high-quality white chocolate (be sure that it contains cocoa butter) and place it in a glass bowl set over simmering water. Stir frequently until the chocolate melts and is smooth. Add it to the warm custard.

SERVING GELATO

As a gelato *purist, I prefer my servings unadorned, except perhaps for an occasional crown of hot fudge or warm caramel sauce. Should you prefer to turn gelato into a more festive affair, here are a few Italian ways of serving it.*

Pass a pitcher of warmed honey for drizzling over the gelato.

Pour a jigger or two of Scotch whiskey or other favorite spirit over the gelato.

Sprinkle the gelato with freshly ground espresso-roast or other dark-roast coffee.

Sweeten fresh berries and/or sliced fruit to taste, then heat in a microwave oven or over medium heat until the fruit is warm and produces juice. Spoon the warm compote over the gelato.

Warm a favorite jam or preserve and spoon over the gelato.

For a coppa mista, scoop three or more flavors of gelato into large goblets or bowls. ❧

147

COFFEE

Purchase high-quality espresso or other dark-roast beans from a reliable source. Whole beans, ground to a fine powder for each cup or pot of coffee, provide the finest taste, although you may opt to have the coffee ground at the time of purchase. To maintain freshness, always buy only the amount you can use in a week's time. Store in an airtight jar.

Authentic espresso can only be made in an espresso maker—electric or nonelectric—and you will need a strong steam spigot for foaming the milk for cappuccino.

To make espresso, use 2 level tablespoons ground coffee per ⅓ cup water. Follow the espresso-machine manufacturer's instructions, dripping the coffee directly into small cups; if made in a coffee pot, distribute the coffee among the espresso cups. A good substitute can easily be prepared in any slow-drip coffee maker. Serve a tiny strip of lemon peel with each cup, if desired.

To make cappuccino, prepare espresso as directed and pour it into a large cup. Follow the espresso-machine manufacturer's instructions for steaming milk. Spoon the foam from steamed milk on top of each cup of espresso and serve immediately; use about half espresso and half milk foam. Offer sweetened cocoa powder or ground cinnamon for dusting the top of each serving.

To make *caffèlatte*, prepare espresso as directed and pour it into a large mug or heatproof glass. Add an equal portion of steamed or heated milk. Top with the foam from steaming the milk, if desired.

CAFFÈ
COFFEE

Whether at home or in stand-up coffee bars, Italians consume good coffee throughout the day. Coffee with hot milk (caffèlatte, also written caffè latte or spelled caffellatte) is the choice for breakfast and the only time that coffee accompanies food. Coffee with steamed milk (cappuccino) is enjoyed all day and into the afternoon. Strong black coffee (caffè or espresso), made from dark, double-roasted beans and usually sweetened with lots of sugar is the choice at the end of a meal and to cap off an evening. (Incidentally, remember that the word is spelled with an s, not an x, thus the correct pronunciation is ess-press-oh.) 🐚

149

LIQUORI E AMARI

AFTER-MEAL DRINKS

Liqueurs have long enjoyed a medicinal reputation among the Italians. They are often credited as digestive aids, or digestivi, along with several bitter, low-alcohol brews known as amari. Whether you choose to serve them at the table or in the living room, alongside coffee or afterward, liquori *extend the pleasure of Italian-style leisurely dining.*

Grappa is a high-alcohol brandy made from the stems and seeds of grapes. It may be served before or after a meal, or stirred into morning or evening coffee. ❧

150

ITALIAN *LIQUORI*
Almond-flavored Amaretto
Anise-laced Anisette and Sambuca
Coffee-based Espresso Liquore
Cherry-flavored Maraschino
Hazelnut-flavored Frangelico
Herb-flavored Galliano
Orange-flavored Tuaca
Vanilla- and herb-flavored Strega
Walnut-flavored Nocello

ITALIAN *AMARI*
Averna
Fernet Branca
Montenegro
Ramazotti
Unicum

Offer an assortment of Italian *liquori* or *amari* at room temperature. Pour into small glasses for sipping. *Sambuca* is usually served with a whole coffee bean in the glass.

MARINATED ROASTED SWEET PEPPERS

A common element of a mixed antipasti, these sweet peppers also make an excellent accompaniment to many second courses such as grilled or roasted poultry, fish, or meat. And they're great on sandwiches of salami, grilled eggplant, or Italian cheese.

152

Minced garlic and chopped fresh basil, oregano, or rosemary may be added along with the marinade. ❧

6 green, red, orange, or golden sweet peppers, or a combination
Salt
Freshly ground black pepper
½ cup extra-virgin olive oil
2 tablespoons freshly squeezed lemon juice
1 tablespoon red wine vinegar or balsamic vinegar

Place the peppers on a grill rack over a charcoal fire, directly over a gas flame, or under a preheated broiler. Roast, turning several times, until the skin is charred on all sides. The timing will depend upon the intensity and proximity of the heat. Transfer the peppers to a paper bag, loosely close the bag, and let stand for about 10 minutes.

Using your fingertips, rub away the charred skin from the peppers; do not rinse. Cut the peppers in half and discard the seeds and membranes. Slice or cut lengthwise into strips and transfer to a shallow bowl or serving platter.

Sprinkle the pepper strips with salt and pepper to taste. Drizzle the oil, lemon juice, and vinegar over the peppers and let stand at room temperature, stirring occasionally to coat evenly in the marinade, for about 30 minutes. The marinated peppers can be covered and refrigerated for up to 1 week.

Makes 6 to 8 servings.

FRESH PASTA DOUGH

About 2 cups all-purpose flour, preferably unbleached
3 or 4 large eggs, at room temperature
1 teaspoon olive oil, preferably extra virgin (optional)
½ teaspoon salt (optional)
All-purpose flour for dusting

To make pasta dough by hand, shape 2 cups flour into a mound on a smooth work surface or in a large, shallow bowl. Place a fist in the center of the mound and move it in a circular motion to spread out the flour and form a wide, shallow well in the center. Add the eggs and the oil and salt, if using, to the well. Using a fork or your fingertips, gently break the egg yolks. Using a circular motion of the fork or with your fingertips, draw the flour from the inside wall of the well and gradually incorporate it into the egg mixture. While mixing with one hand, use your free hand to keep the wall of flour intact.

When the eggs are no longer runny, push most of the flour over them, reserving to one side any flour you think will not be necessary. Knead the dough with both hands until it forms a crumbly mass. If the dough feels too sticky, gradually work in more flour. If it is too dry and crumbly, work in a few drops of water at a time until it seems moist enough.

Position the dough to one side of the work surface and scrape off all bits of flour and egg from the work surface with a flat metal dough scraper or a knife blade. Wash and dry your hands, then lightly sprinkle them and the work surface with the same type of flour used in the dough. Place the dough in the center of the flour-dusted area and knead by pressing down on it with the heels of your palms. Fold the dough in half over itself, give it a half turn, and repeat this kneading procedure until the dough feels very elastic and smooth and doesn't break apart when you pull it, 10 to 12 minutes. Knead in additional flour as necessary. Test the dough by inserting a finger into the center. If it comes out dry and clean, the dough has enough flour incorporated; if the finger is moist or has dough attached, more flour is required.

Shape the dough into a ball and dust it lightly with flour. Wrap in plastic wrap or cover with an inverted bowl and let stand at room temperature for at least 25 minutes or up to 2 hours to allow it to relax.

After the dough rests, roll out and cut as directed in individual recipes.

To make pasta dough in a food processor, combine the eggs and the oil and salt, if using, in the bowl fitted with a metal blade and pulse until well mixed. Add 1¾ cups of the flour and run the machine until the dough gathers together into a ball. Add as much remaining flour as necessary to form a dough that doesn't feel too sticky. Transfer to a lightly floured surface and knead by hand as described in the hand method. Form into a ball and let rest as directed.

Makes about 1 pound, enough for 8 servings as a pasta course, or 4 servings as a main course.

BASICS

PASTA FRESCA
FRESH PASTA DOUGH

All-purpose flour yields the most tender pasta. Semolina flour, sometimes sold as pasta flour, is best left for making commercial dried pasta products.

Italian pasta makers do not traditionally add oil or salt to their pasta dough, but I like the added flavor. Nor do they generally add seasonings or colorings, other than spinach, except in the Piedmont region where they sometimes add vegetables such as beet or tomato to the dough. To achieve these colors and flavors, add about 1 cup vegetable purée along with the eggs. If you wish to be more adventuresome, please see my Pasta Cookbook. ❦

153

BASIL SAUCE, GENOA STYLE

PESTO ALLA GENOVESE

BASIL SAUCE, GENOA STYLE

In Liguria, the birthplace of this heaven-sent mixture, pecorino fiore sardo is the cheese of choice. Since only harsher-tasting pecorino romano is available here, I prefer the sauce made with milder and nuttier Parmigiano-Reggiano. I sometimes make the sauce with almonds, walnuts, or even pecans, and the touch of vinegar in this version is also nontraditional. Some Genoese recipes also call for about 3 tablespoons softened unsalted butter to be stirred in with the cheese.

Use pesto to crown pasta, pizza, or grilled bread; stir it into soups or risotto; serve it alongside grilled fish; or spread it on sandwiches. The sauce should never be cooked or heated, but tossed with pasta or added to other dishes at the time of serving. ❦

2 cups firmly packed fresh basil leaves, rinsed and dried
¼ cup pine nuts
2 or 3 garlic cloves, peeled
1 teaspoon red wine vinegar or balsamic vinegar (optional)
½ cup extra-virgin olive oil
¾ cup freshly grated parmesan cheese (about 3 ounces), preferably
   Parmigiano-Reggiano, or a mixture of ½ cup parmesan and
   ¼ cup *pecorino romano* cheeses
About ¼ teaspoon salt

Combine the basil, pine nuts, garlic, and vinegar (if used) in a food processor fitted with a metal blade or in a blender and chop finely. With the motor running, slowly add the oil, continuing to blend until well mixed. Transfer to a bowl, stir in the cheese, and season to taste with salt. Alternatively (and traditionally), grind the basil, pine nuts, and garlic in a mortar with a pestle before working in the remaining ingredients.

Use immediately, or transfer to a container, cover with a thin film of olive oil to keep the sauce from darkening, and refrigerate for up to 3 days. To freeze for as long as 6 months, omit the cheese during preparation and add it after thawing the pesto.

Makes about ¾ cup.

TOMATO SAUCE

½ cup olive oil, preferably extra-virgin, or ½ cup (1 stick)
  unsalted butter
1 cup finely chopped yellow onion
1 cup finely chopped carrot
1 cup finely chopped celery or fennel
2 teaspoons minced or pressed garlic, or to taste
4 cups peeled, seeded, drained, and chopped ripe or canned plum tomato
1 teaspoon sugar, or to taste
Salt

In a saucepan, heat the oil or butter over medium-high heat. Add the onion, carrot, and celery or fennel and sauté until soft and lightly golden, about 5 minutes. Add the garlic and sauté for 1 minute longer. Stir in the tomatoes, sugar, and salt to taste. Reduce the heat to low and simmer, uncovered, until thick, about 30 minutes. Use immediately, or cover and refrigerate for up to 4 or 5 days. Reheat before using.

For a smoother sauce, transfer to a food processor fitted with a metal blade or to a blender and purée. Pour into a clean saucepan and reheat before using.

Makes about 4 cups.

MAYONNAISE

2 egg yolks
About 2 tablespoons freshly squeezed lemon juice
About 1 teaspoon salt
1 to 1½ cups olive oil, preferably extra-virgin

In a food processor fitted with a metal blade or in a blender, combine the egg yolks and lemon juice and salt to taste. Blend a few seconds. With the motor running, gradually add the oil in a slow, steady trickle. Blend until thick and creamy. Adjust salt and lemon juice to taste. Transfer to a container, cover, and refrigerate until ready to use.

Makes about 1 cup.

GARLIC VARIATION

Add 2 garlic cloves, or to taste, to the egg yolks, lemon juice, and salt. Blend until the garlic is puréed.

SALSA DI POMODORO

TOMATO SAUCE

*D*uring tomato season, make quantities of this sauce and freeze for winter use. Whenever flavorful summer tomatoes are unavailable, canned plum tomatoes make a much better sauce than out-of-season supermarket varieties. If you like, add minced fresh or crumbled dried herbs or minced fresh or crushed dried hot chile to taste. ❧

155

MAIONESE

MAYONNAISE

*I*talian-style mayonnaise has the rich flavor of olive oil. It will keep for up to a week in the refrigerator. ❧

BALSAMIC SAUCE

BASICS

SALSA DI BALSAMICO

BALSAMIC SAUCE

For making this long-simmered sauce, choose less expensive factory-made balsamic vinegar and save the vintage version for salads. I've opted to thicken the sauce by adding a little cornstarch dissolved in cold water during the final heating, a method advocated by some modern chefs; if you prefer a thinner sauce, omit the cornstarch. For a thicker, richer, more classical sauce, stir about a cup of demi-glace *(highly concentrated meat stock) into the sauce before beginning the final reduction.*

The sauce is wonderful with roasted or braised meats. ❧

3 tablespoons unsalted butter
2 pounds veal, lamb, chicken, or game bones, or a combination
3 ounces Italian bacon (*pancetta*), chopped
⅔ cup chopped yellow onion
⅔ cup chopped celery
⅔ cup chopped carrot
6 fresh parsley sprigs, preferably flat-leaf type
4 fresh thyme sprigs
1 bay leaf
1 cup balsamic vinegar
3 ⅔ cups dry white wine
9 cups Italian-Style Broth (page 157), made from meat or game,
    or 9 cups canned beef or chicken broth, preferably low-sodium type
1 cup tomato purée
1 teaspoon juniper berries, crushed
12 whole black peppercorns, crushed
1 cup dry red wine
1 tablespoon cornstarch dissolved in 1 tablespoon cold water
2 tablespoons unsalted butter for serving
Salt

In a large stockpot, melt the butter over medium-high heat. Add the bones, *pancetta*, onion, celery, and carrot and sauté until the meat and vegetables are well browned, about 10 minutes. Add the parsley, thyme, and bay leaf and sauté for about 2 minutes longer. Drain off and discard the fat from the pan.

Add the vinegar and ⅔ cup of the white wine, place over high heat, and deglaze the pan by scraping to dislodge any browned bits on the bottom and sides. Cook until the liquids evaporate completely, leaving a caramelized residue on the pan bottom. Stir in 8 cups (2 quarts) of the broth and the remaining 3 cups white wine, reduce the heat to medium-low, and bring to a simmer, skimming off any scum that rises to the surface. Reduce the heat to low, cover, and cook for 3 hours, occasionally skimming away any scum that rises to the surface.

Stir in the tomato purée, juniper berries, and peppercorns. Simmer for about 15 minutes. Strain through a *chinois* or a sieve lined with cheesecloth into a clean saucepan, pressing against the solids to release as much liquid as possible. Add the red wine and the remaining 1 cup broth. Place over low heat and bring to a simmer, skimming away any scum from the surface. Cook, uncovered, until reduced to about 2½ cups, about 30 minutes.

Strain the sauce through a *chinois* or cheesecloth-lined sieve into a clean saucepan. (The sauce may be made 1 or 2 days ahead up to this point and refrigerated.) Place over medium heat and bring to a gentle boil. Add the dissolved cornstarch and the 2 tablespoons butter and stir until the butter is melted and the sauce is thickened to a syrupy consistency, 2 to 3 minutes. Season to taste with salt. Serve warm.

Makes about 2½ cups.

ITALIAN-STYLE BROTH

3 pounds lean beef or veal meat; 4 to 5 pounds chicken, duck, turkey,
  or other poultry parts, including bony pieces such as necks, backs, and
  wings (do not add liver); or a combination of meat and poultry
2 pounds beef or veal bones, if making meat broth
1 yellow onion, quartered
1 large carrot, peeled and cut into chunks
2 celery stalks, cut into pieces
5 or 6 fresh parsley sprigs, preferably flat-leaf type
About 1 tablespoon salt

Quickly rinse the meat or poultry and the bones (if used) under cold running water.
Place on a cutting surface and cut off and discard excess fat.

In a large stockpot, combine the meat or poultry, bones (if used), onion, carrot,
celery, and parsley sprigs. Add enough cold water to cover by about 2 inches. Place
over medium heat and bring just to a boil. Reduce the heat to low, cover, and
simmer until well flavored, about 3 hours. Use a slotted utensil or wire skimmer to
remove any foamy scum that rises to the surface; there will be more of this scum
during the early stages of cooking. During the last hour of cooking, add salt to taste
and remove the cover.

When done, remove from heat and let cool for a few minutes.

Line a colander or sieve with several layers of dampened cheesecloth and place in a
large bowl. Strain the slightly cooled broth through the colander into the bowl,
pressing against the vegetables and meat to release all the liquid. Discard the bones,
meat, vegetables, and herbs. Refrigerate the warm broth, uncovered, until cold,
then cover tightly until well chilled, preferably overnight.

When the broth is well chilled, remove any fat that has solidified on the surface.
Reheat the broth and use immediately, or cover and refrigerate for up to 4 days, or
freeze for up to 6 months. Reheat to boiling before using.

Makes about 2 quarts.

SAUCE VARIATION

For a thin, low-fat sauce for pasta or other dishes, reduce the strained broth by half
over high heat, then strain and reduce by half once or twice more before chilling
and defatting.

BRODO

ITALIAN-STYLE BROTH

*I*talian cooks prefer a lighter broth
than the richer, more flavorful stock
favored by the French. ❦

POLENTA

POLENTA

Polenta is the Italian name for both the cornmeal and the cooked mush. The finished dish may be served freshly cooked as a side dish or as a bed for cooked meats. Frequently it is cooled, then sliced or cut into fanciful shapes and reheated for serving as a side dish or used as a component in other dishes. ❦

Italian kitchen tradition calls for continuous stirring of barely simmering polenta for about 45 minutes. This revolutionary version is based on methods used by today's chefs and yields the same creamy results with much less attention.

For directions on making soft polenta, please see recipe on page 68.

8 cups (2 quarts) Italian-Style Broth (page 157); canned chicken or vegetable broth, preferably reduced-sodium type; or water
1 tablespoon salt, or to taste
2 cups cornmeal (see sidebar page 159)

OPTIONAL ADDITIONS
½ cup (1 stick) unsalted butter
⅔ cup freshly grated parmesan cheese (about 3 ounces), preferably Parmigiano-Reggiano
2 cups freshly shredded good-melting cheese such as Fontina or crumbled Gorgonzola or goat's milk cheese
2 tablespoons minced fresh herb of choice, or 2 teaspoons crumbled dried herb of choice
1 cup sautéed fresh wild mushrooms such as porcini or chanterelles
1 cup chopped cooked spinach, Swiss chard, or other green
¼ cup minced drained sun-dried tomatoes packed in olive oil

Unsalted butter or extra-virgin olive oil if panfrying, grilling, broiling, or roasting

Select a large metal bowl that will fit over a larger pot to create a double boiler arrangement or use a large double boiler. Fill the bottom pot with water, keeping the level well below the bottom of the insert. Bring the water to a simmer.

Meanwhile, combine the broth or water and salt in the top portion of the double boiler. Using a wire whisk or wooden spoon, stir the water in one direction to create a whirlpool in the center. Slowly drizzle a thin stream of the polenta into the center of the swirling water until completely mixed and smooth.

Cover the polenta container tightly with foil and set it over the simmering water, being certain that the bottom of the polenta container sits well above the water. Cook, uncovering and using a rubber spatula to scrape the bottom and sides of the container several times, until the polenta is thick and smooth, 1½ to 2 hours.

Remove from the heat and, if desired, stir in any one or a compatible combination of the suggested additions. Stir until the butter or cheese melts, if using.

To serve warm, pour the mixture onto a platter or other flat surface and smooth the top with a damp wooden spoon. Alternatively, pour the polenta into a bowl that has been dampened with water, then unmold onto a serving plate. Cut polenta into wedges and serve immediately.

For polenta that is to be reheated later or used in other dishes, after adding any selected additions as directed above, pour the hot mixture into a generously buttered 5-by-9-inch loaf pan, a 9-by-13-inch baking pan, or a 9-inch round cake pan. Cool to room temperature, then cover and refrigerate for at least 2 hours or as long as 3 days. Turn the chilled loaf out onto a cutting surface and slice or cut into fanciful shapes. Use as directed in recipes or panfry in butter or olive oil. You can also brush the slices on both sides with melted butter or olive oil and heat them on a grill rack over a medium-hot fire, under a preheated broiler, or in a preheated 450°F oven until crispy on the outside and heated through.

Makes 6 servings.

WHITE SAUCE

5 tablespoons unsalted butter
5 tablespoons all-purpose flour
3 cups milk
Salt
Freshly ground white pepper
Freshly grated nutmeg (optional)

In a heavy-bottom saucepan, melt the butter over low heat. Add the flour and whisk briskly to blend until smooth; do not brown. Add the milk all at once and whisk until very smooth. Season to taste with salt, pepper, and nutmeg (if used). Simmer, stirring frequently, until thickened to the consistency of heavy cream, about 10 minutes.

Use immediately, or cover and set aside for up to 2 hours and gently reheat before using.

Makes about 3 cups.

*A*lthough in the United States we identify Italian cornmeal with the coarse yellow variety sold here as polenta, in Italy the type of cornmeal varies with the region. Finely ground yellow or white cornmeal is favored in the Veneto; a coarser yellow meal is preferred in Piedmont and Lombardy. ❧

159

SALSA BESCIAMELLA
WHITE SAUCE

*A*n essential ingredient in many lasagna and cannelloni preparations, this smooth sauce also makes a rich-tasting pasta sauce containing less fat than cream-based toppings. ❧

FLATBREAD

FOCACCIA
FLATBREAD

The directions are for use with a heavy-duty standing electric mixer, which makes and kneads the dough in only a few minutes. Alternatively, the dough may be mixed in a bowl by hand or in a heavy-duty food processor, then kneaded on a lightly floured surface until it is smooth and elastic.

160

In high-humidity environments, you may need up to 4 cups flour to achieve a smooth dough. ❧

1 tablespoon sugar
1½ cups warm (110° to 115°F) water
1 envelope (¼ ounce) active dry yeast
3¼ cups unbleached all-purpose flour
2 teaspoons salt
Extra-virgin olive oil
Kosher salt or coarse sea salt

In a small bowl, dissolve the sugar in the warm water. Sprinkle the yeast over the water and stir gently until it dissolves, about 1 minute. Let stand in a warm spot until a thin layer of creamy foam covers the surface, about 5 minutes, indicating the yeast is effective. (Discard the mixture and start over with a fresh package of yeast if bubbles have not formed within 5 minutes.)

In the bowl of a heavy-duty standing electric mixer, combine 3 cups of the flour, the salt, and the yeast mixture. Attach the flat beater, gradually turn on the machine to the medium speed, and beat until well mixed, about 1 minute. Replace the flat beater with the dough hook and knead at medium speed until the dough is smooth and elastic, about 5 minutes. Pinch off a piece of dough and feel it. If it is sticky, continue kneading while gradually adding just enough of the remaining ¼ cup flour for the dough to lose its stickiness. If the dough is dry and crumbly, add warm water, a tablespoon at a time, until the dough is smooth and elastic.

Pour a little olive oil into a bowl and generously grease the bottom and sides. Shape the dough into a ball and place it in the bowl, turning the dough to coat completely on all sides with oil. Cover the bowl tightly with plastic wrap to prevent moisture loss, and set aside to rise in a draft-free warm place (75°F to 89°F—a hotter environment may kill the yeast) until tripled in bulk, about 3 hours.

Preheat an oven to 375°F. Pour about 2 tablespoons olive oil into a 9-by-13-inch pan and generously grease the bottom and sides.

Punch down the dough and place it in the center of the prepared pan. Using your fingertips, spread the dough to fit the bottom of the pan evenly; it may be springy and a bit difficult to spread. Using a finger, poke deep holes in the top of the dough to create a dimpled effect. Generously brush the dough all over with olive oil and sprinkle with the coarse salt.

Bake until golden brown, 30 to 35 minutes.

Remove to a wire rack and let cool in the pan for about 5 minutes. Turn out onto the wire rack and cool about 10 minutes longer. Cut into squares or rectangles or as directed in recipes.

Makes 6 servings.

CANDIED ORANGE ZEST

4 to 6 oranges
3 cups water
1 cup sugar
⅓ cup freshly squeezed orange juice

Using a vegetable peeler, remove the zest (the colored part of the peel with none of the bitter white pith) from the oranges. Reserve the oranges for another use. Slice the zest into enough long, thin strips to measure 1 cup; set aside.

Pour the water into a saucepan and bring to a boil over medium-high heat. Add the orange zest, reduce the heat to low, and simmer, uncovered, for about 10 minutes. Drain the orange zest, then spread on paper toweling. Use additional paper toweling to pat the zest dry.

In a small saucepan, combine the sugar and orange juice. Place over medium heat until the sugar melts. Add the reserved orange zest and cook, uncovered, stirring frequently, until the zest is well glazed, about 15 minutes. Using a slotted utensil, transfer the zest to a wire rack set over aluminum foil to drain.

When the zest is cold and drained, use immediately or transfer to a storage container, cover tightly, and refrigerate for up to several weeks.

Makes about 1 cup.

SCORZA CANDITO D'ARANCIA

CANDIED ORANGE ZEST

Freshly candied citrus zest tastes far superior to commercial preparations. Select the best unblemished fruit you can find. Use the same technique for glazing the zest of citron (a thick-skinned Italian citrus fruit), grapefruit, lemon, lime, or tangerine.

In addition to its use in Sienese Spice Cake (page 127) and Chocolate-Glazed Almond Cookies (page 131), the zest is delicious on ice cream, as a sweet snack, or as a garnish for cakes and other desserts. ❧

161

RECIPE INDEX

INDEX TO ITALIAN DISHES IN OTHER JAMES McNAIR COOKBOOKS

TABLE OF EQUIVALENTS

The exact equivalents in the following tables have been rounded for convenience.

US/UK

oz = ounce
lb = pound
in = inch
ft = foot
tbl = tablespoon
fl oz = fluid ounce
qt = quart

METRIC

g = gram
kg = kilogram
mm = millimeter
cm = centimeter
ml = milliliter
l = liter

WEIGHTS

US/UK	Metric
1 oz	30 g
2 oz	60 g
3 oz	90 g
4 oz (¼ lb)	125 g
5 oz (⅓ lb)	155 g
6 oz	185 g
7 oz	220 g
8 oz (½ lb)	250 g
10 oz	315 g
12 oz ¾ lb)	75 g
14 oz	40 g
16 oz (1 lb)	500 g
1 ½ lb	750 g
2 lb	kg
3 lb	5 kg

OVEN TEMPERATURES

Fahrenheit	Celsius	Gas
250	120	1/2
275	140	1
300	150	2
325	160	3
350	180	4
375	190	5
400	200	6
425	220	7
450	230	8
475	240	9
500	260	10

LIQUIDS

US	Metric	UK
2 tbl	30 ml	1 fl oz
¼ cup	60 ml	2 fl oz
⅓ cup	80 ml	3 fl oz
½ cup	125 ml	4 fl oz
⅔ cup	60 ml	5 fl oz
¾ cup	180 ml	6 fl oz
1 cup	250 ml	8 fl oz
1 ½ cups	375 ml	12 fl oz
2 cups	500 ml	16 fl oz
4 cups/1 qt	1 l	32 fl oz

LENGTH MEASURES

⅛ in	3 mm
¼ in	6 mm
½ in	12 mm
1 in	2.5 cm
2 in	5 cm
3 in	7.5 cm
4 in	10 cm
5 in	13 cm
6 in	15 cm
7 in	18 cm
8 in	20 cm
9 in	23 cm
10 in	25 cm
11 in	28 cm
12/1 ft	30 cm

All-Purpose (Plain) Flour/ Dried Bread Crumbs/Chopped Nuts

¼ cup	1 oz	30 g
⅓ cup	1 ½ oz	45 g
½ cup	2 oz	60 g
¾ cup	3 oz	90 g
1 cup	4 oz	125 g
1 ½ cups	6 oz	185 g
2 cups	8 oz	250 g

Whole-Wheat (Wholemeal) Flour

3 tbl	1 oz	30 g
½ cup	2 oz	60 g
⅔ cup	3 oz	90 g
1 cup	4 oz	125 g
1 ¼ cups	5 oz	155 g
1 ⅔ cups	7 oz	210 g
1 ¾ cups	8 oz	250 g

White Sugar

¼ cup	2 oz	60 g
⅓ cup	3 oz	90 g
½ cup	4 oz	125 g
¾ cup	6 oz	185 g
1 cup	8 oz	250 g
1 ½ cups	12 oz	375 g
2 cups	1 lb	500 g

Raisins/Currants/Semolina

¼ cup	1 oz	30 g
⅓ cup	2 oz	60 g
½ cup	3 oz	90 g
¾ cup	4 oz	125 g
1 cup	5 oz	155 g

Rice/Cornmeal

⅓ cup	2 oz	60 g
½ cup	2 ½ oz	75 g
3/4 cup	4 oz	125 g
1 cup	5 oz	155 g
1 ½ cups	8 oz	250 g

Dried Beans

¼ cup	1 ½oz	45 g
⅓ cup	2 oz	60 g
½ cup	3 oz	90 g
¾ cup	5 oz	155 g
1 cup	6 oz	185 g
1 ¼ cups	8 oz	250 g
1 ½ cups	12 oz	375 g

Honey

2 tbl	2 oz	60 g
¼ cup	3 oz	90 g
½ cup	5 oz	155 g
¾ cup	8 oz	250 g
1 cup	11 oz	345 g

Grated Parmesan/Romano Cheese

¼ cup	1 oz	30 g
½ cup	2 oz	60 g
¾ cup	3 oz	90 g
1 cup	4 oz	125 g
1 ⅓ cups	5 oz	155 g
2 cups	7 oz	220 g

RECIPES WERE TESTED BY:

Antonia Allegra
John Carr
Martha Casselman
Chris Cook
Rick Dinihanian
Ruth Dosher
Jan Ellis
Mark Forbert
Carol Gallagher
Naila Gallagher
Louis Hicks
Gail High
Steven Holden
Sal Katzowitz
Connie Landry
John Lyle
Meri McEneny
J. O. McNair
Lucille McNair
Martha McNair
Marian May
Maile Moore
Sandra Moore
Jack Porter
John Richardson
Julie Schaper
Diana Sheehan
Michele Sordi
Brooksley Spence
Kristi Spence

168

ACKNOWLEDGMENTS

To everyone at Chronicle Books for their continued good work.

To Sharon Silva for her valued expertise as copy editor.

To Marian May and Mimma Foggi for contributing to my research and providing inspiration and sound advice.

To Iris Fuller and her sensational staff at Fillamento, the world's most innovative store, for the generous loan of mountains of merchandise.

To Rick Dinihanian and John Lyle of Green Lizard Design, dear friends and excellent neighbors, for creating an exciting look for this book.

To my family and friends who are always there when I need them, and who allow me not always to be there when I'm immersed in a book. Special thanks to Martha McNair for accompanying me on long prop-shopping expeditions and to John Carr and Jack Porter for sharing their San Francisco homes.

To Beauregard Ezekiel Valentine, Joshua J. Chew, Michael T. Wigglebutt, Dweasel Pickle, Miss Vivien "Bunny" Fleigh, and Miss Olivia de Pusspuss for eagerly anticipating each new dish as it was developed.

And to Andrew Moore for his creative ideas, expert assistance, and constant caring.